# 24 HOURS TO YOUR NEXT JOB, RAISE, OR PROMOTION

# CAREER COACH

# 24 HOURS TO YOUR NEXT JOB, RAISE, OR PROMOTION

## ROBIN RYAN

John Wiley & Sons, Inc.

*New York • Chichester • Weinheim • Brisbane • Singapore • Toronto*

This text is printed on acid-free paper.

Copyright © 1997 by Robin Ryan
Published by John Wiley & Sons, Inc.

This publication is designed to provide accurate and authoritative information in regard to the subject matter covered. It is sold with the understanding that the publisher is not engaged in rendering legal, accounting, or other professional services. If legal advice or other expert assistance is required, the services of a competent professional person should be sought.

ISBN: 0-417-19066-7

Printed in the United States of America
10 9 8 7 6 5 4 3 2 1

*To my husband Steven,
whose partnership enriches my life*

*To Sophie, Jordan, and Lillie Grace—
may you grow up and find careers
that are immensely satisfying*

# CAN THIS BOOK HELP YOU?

A bsolutely. Whether you're a manager, a secretary, a high-level executive, or a recent college graduate, these proven techniques are solid guidance for anyone who wants to manage his or her career. Here's a list of those it can help:

✔ Anyone looking for a better job

✔ Someone planning their career or looking for a promotion

✔ Anyone who wants a raise

✔ Individuals who want to negotiate a higher salary

The entire process is here, but it all comes down to this: Use the 24 hours before your big interview or meeting with the employer to prepare and create the appropriate tools that market your value. Then deliver the message, in a confident way, that *you* are the *best* one to perform the job and should rightfully be paid your full value to do it.

That's all you need to do to succeed, and this book will be your guide.

# CONTENTS

# ACKNOWLEDGMENTS

Careers are shaped and formed, and mine has been influenced by so many. I'm thankful to KIRO-TV, KOMO Radio, and the *Seattle Times* for supporting me in my quest to help people find more satisfying and rewarding jobs. I'm grateful to those who influenced my speaking business—Tracy White, Ed Lincoln, Jeff Rowoth—all three gave me a special opportunity at their associations and colleges to help people find jobs.

So many individuals provided assistance on this book. An endless list of clients, top executives, and HR managers offered their insights and stories—to all of them I'm grateful. Specifically, I received notable assistance from Peg Kowalik, Bob Holman, Chris Slattery, Jim Mullen, Sandy DeHan, Tracy White, Annette Slattery, Jim Medzegian—all of whom I acknowledge with a big thank you. Most particularly, Steve Ryan made valuable suggestions and offered terrific ideas that truly aided in improving this book.

Mike Hamilton, my editor at Wiley, must be credited with suggesting I write this book. I'm blessed with by far the best agent in the world—Shelly Roth.

Dawnie Thompson and Adam Zoll were two of my biggest assets, as they typed, edited, and formatted each word of this manuscript.

Finally, I must thank God, who seemed to work through me as I wrote each page and provided a continuous flow of solid information and ideas to meet my objective—to teach others effective ways to find better, more enriching positions. My road of writing three books at one time (I also worked on *Winning Resumés* and *Winning Cover Letters* during this same six months) has been unique, demanding, and hopefully one that achieves my personal goal: to help you find a better position, one where you are happily paid what you are worth.

# GETTING THE MOST FROM THIS BOOK

I've written this book in a coaching format in the hope that you will get the same motivation and encouragement I offer clients in an actual career counseling session. You'll also learn the vital facts, trends, market strategies, and tools necessary to land a new job, obtain a promotion, and get paid what you are worth. This career resource guide has a detailed table of contents so you can quickly proceed to the specific area that will help you the most with your goal. Chapter 4 discusses in depth the communication tools, or "persuasion" tools as I call them, that have aided thousands of my career counseling clients and seminar participants to move their careers on to more rewarding positions. This key chapter will benefit every reader. Also, Chapter 3 will aid you in determining your strongest skills and identifying the ideal job and company you would like to work for. These skill assessment exercises are the foundation of your persuasion tools, so be sure to complete that chapter.

The book is laced with client and employer stories and insights to give you a firsthand look at how employers and employees (or job candidates) operate in real life. Their stories are all true, with only personal and company names changed to preserve their confidentiality. The insights you learn from their interactions should be very enlightening! The market-tested techniques will save you endless hours of frustration and disappointment.

The workplace is constantly changing. I've been brutally honest about what works, what doesn't, and the effort needed to succeed, including the new hiring methodology, career trends that reshape the workplace, and the profiles you need to effectively market yourself today, tomorrow, and in the years to come.

One client summed it up best when he told me: "It is absolutely astounding to me the difference the right tools and words made in my search for employment. I learned so much from you that will allow me to never be that low, even if I'm unemployed again. I know now I have a great deal to offer an employer, and I've learned how to appropriately package it."

Welcome to your personal career coaching session. Together, we can and will positively change your life.

# 24 HOURS TO YOUR NEXT JOB, RAISE, OR PROMOTION

# DREAM BIG!

## DARE TO DREAM

*How can you be true to your future if you don't know what it holds? Good question! Although the future is unpredictable, everyone can have a direct influence on how things turn out. The most successful individuals understand the importance of having a plan that will help them accomplish their dreams. Unfortunately, a majority of individuals seem to exist on a day-to-day basis. To these people, life consists of "marking time."*

*Although planning for the future is always tentative, without a plan there is less chance of a dream coming true. Thus it is important when planning your future to include some high expectations, even though they may appear slightly out of reach. If you do not set your goals high, you may miss out on some great life experiences.*

*—ANONYMOUS*

"This job is a dream come true! To most people it would look like another sales position with another big company. But to me, it's perfect," said 50-year-old Andy, one of my career counseling clients. "I beat out 2,000 applicants—30 that made it to the interview stage—now I'm their regional sales manager! My meeting with you was brief, just one day before my initial interview. You helped me gain the confidence that I could be competitive. You felt I was well qualified, and we reaffirmed my top selling points. That was very important to me—the self-marketing for myself is pretty difficult. *I got it, I got it*—I can barely believe it—but if you're a pilot like I am, there are only a handful of jobs selling pleasure planes in America. Now, one of them is mine," he said.

Andy had a passion—he loved to fly and show people the wonders above the ground. When he lost his sales job for a major airplane maker due to a reorganization, he was devastated. The derailment was tough, and personally he feared he'd never, *ever,* find that kind of great job again. At 50, he felt the good life was over. He avoided airports at all cost; it was just too painful. Then he got wind of a new plane being designed by a prominent airplane maker, and that led to uncovering a potential sales job. He applied. After the initial interview he was invited to corporate headquarters for a couple days of testing and interviews. An hour before he was to leave for the airport, his father-in-law died. When he called the company, they told him they had hired a consultant to do an evaluation and that he would have to come within two days to be considered. He went. They gave him a videotaped test of an angry customer and another of a disgruntled employee, both of which went well. The third test involved an "in-box" with a stack of memos and notes. Andy had to decide how to handle them. He felt that it did not go well. He returned home and waited. He finally got a call from John, the company manager, who told Andy he'd flunked the "in-box" test—the results indicated he was disorganized. But Andy did not take that failure as a "no" answer. He sat down and composed a well-crafted, two-page letter to persuade John, the hiring manager, that not only was he well organized, but he was a good salesman. John later commented on one line that read, "I'm not used to flunking tests! I have had success at everything from carrier landings to getting an MBA." Andy then went on to quote his sales record and paint a detailed picture of how organized he keeps his home-office with A, B, and C in-boxes. He told John about the numerous computerized programs he used to track and keep up with the hundreds of clients he had at his previous job. The employer was convinced. The letter resulted in another phone call. Finally, Andy got the job. In *24 Hours,* he went from losing the job to landing it. The letter (and, of course, his track record) really convinced them. He got his dream job. He told me, "I feel like the candy man. I can make other people's dreams—the fantasy of owning an airplane—come true. There's no better job in the world for me than this."

There is no end to the possibilities you can reach as you navigate your career. You want to run a department? You can do it. You'd like to be president of a company? Obtainable. You want a better company to work for? Easy. You desire a higher salary and better perks? No problem. Together, using this book, we will set the goals, create the action plans, and develop your persuasion package (the communications tools) to convince employers to hand you your dreams. You define what you want and learn the success strategies to get it. The more you strive for, the more you'll get. The only person who can stop you is you. Forget the economy—my clients are landing terrific jobs every day. Achieving personal satisfaction is our objective. Dream BIG!

## *Just 24 Hours*

✔ *24 Hours* to prepare and convince an employer to hire you

✔ *24 Hours* to prepare and pitch your employer for a raise

✔ *24 Hours* to land the promotion you've been dreaming of

HOW? Skeptical? It can't be true. . . . *Can it?*

For 18 years I've researched the employment field, hired employees, coached, and taught job search and hiring seminars. I've learned the proven strategies and techniques that *work.* I've used them personally, and hundreds of my career counseling clients have used them with great success, as have seminar participants such as Susan, who wrote to say, "Robin, your techniques and methods really work. Both my husband and I used them, and not only did we get in the door, we got jobs!" Throughout this book, I will share those winning techniques with you. Usually you have only 24 Hours before your big interview or management meeting. I'll show you how to maximize your efforts. You'll learn how to create your "persuasion package" to make the meeting or interview go your way. You'll learn the exact words, actions, and phrases that convince employers. I've covered the techniques, the tools, and the actual words and dialogue to allow you to easily apply this information to your own situation. You're about to develop the self-confidence, as well as specific tools (The Hiring Chart™, 60 Second Sell™, 5 Point Agenda™, Productivity Monitor™, Salary Extractor™), to make success happen for you. These tools are proven and effective.

**Dream big.** *A day can make a huge difference!*

## *What's Stopping You?*

### Career Killer #1: Fear of Failure

Many people remain in a stagnant or unsatisfying position. Why? They are afraid. Fear can cause a powerful paralysis. No one welcomes rejection, but fear may be all that stands in the way of you and your dreams. Catherine, a 33-year-old grants administrator, spent six years in a nonprofit organization where the job grew to be boring. She thought of looking for a new job, but nagging doubts held her back: *What if no one hires*

**Fear is really the culprit that prevents many from finding better jobs or asking to be paid what they are truly worth.**

me? What if it's worse than this? What if I don't like the people? I won't get three weeks vacation.

Then one day Catherine saw an ad for a terrific job at American Express. We worked on her resumé and cover letter. She mailed them in and got the interview. She went to the meeting with her persuasion package ready. She got the job and, unbelievably (at least to her), she also got a $5,000 salary increase. Not only did she land the job over hundreds of other candidates, she negotiated a higher salary than they initially offered. Catherine had spent two years thinking about leaving. Nothing changed until the day she overcame her fear and pushed forward.

If you don't try, you'll never succeed. Don't let fear spoil what could be a terrific and better future for you.

## Career Killer #2: Listening to Others

Your spouse, colleagues, parents, or friends don't always know what's best for you. One client held a job that enmeshed her in some terrible office politics. Too many days she went to work with anxiety and came home frustrated, even in tears. Her husband blamed her. "It's your fault," he said. "You can't get along with others. It's you; you're the problem." He only added to her pain, hurt, and lowered her self-esteem. One day, after a bad confrontation at work, she made a decision. She would quit. Good-bye state job, good-bye lifetime security and good benefits. Good-bye daily pressure, anxiety, and frustration. Her husband was not too supportive; he never wanted her to quit her job. But she had listened to him for an entire year while she endured that job. When it got worse, he still expected her to stay and just "live with it." It was a difficult time in her life. She worked hard to find a new job in an environment where she could thrive. It took six months. Today she's a customer service manager at a growing company that values her as an employee and has promoted her twice.

It can be difficult and lonely to make career choices. It does not always turn out as you plan. A merger, a downsize, or a new boss can redirect or detour a great job. In the end, only *you* are responsible for your career. Your friends and spouse may have good intentions, but they don't walk in your shoes. Listen to yourself. Your dreams and your goals are all that matter. Don't pay any attention to those well-meaning naysayers who warn you that you can't do it. You can!

## Career Killer #3: Seeking Job Security

Job security is dead. It does not exist inside a company; even government agencies have begun to downsize. I remember a man in my job search class. He took numerous vocational tests and had a strong background from the Navy in electronics. Yet he kept saying he was going to go to work for the post office. It was secure. No one was going to fire him. It took him 16 months, but he got hired by the post office, where he stayed in the same low-level job for the rest of his career. He did not have a high level of job satisfaction, and he never moved ahead. But he was "secure." Today, job security is something you build for yourself. It exists inside you.

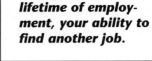

*It is your skills, talents, and abilities that will ensure your lifetime of employment, your ability to find another job.*

Upon completing this book, you'll have gained the needed insight into today's (and tomorrow's) workplace to shape your decisions. You must now be an effective manager of your career and professional growth. The tools and strategies you will learn will enable you to move on whenever you need to or want to. Labor studies estimate you'll have over 10 job changes during your working lifetime. You ensure your future by developing a strong set of skills and a good self-marketing ability.

## Career Killer #4: Don't Know How

Moving ahead requires both risk and initiative. Many people get stymied because they don't see exactly how to get ahead. This book will help you define some goals and lay out a path. You should also learn more about the career options and paths in your current field or in a new field. Join a professional association. It'll broaden your exposure and allow you to develop mentor relationships and new professional friends to gain clearer insight. There are over 25,000 associations throughout America. Most fields have a professional club. Check with your library and look up a resource entitled the *Encyclopedia of Associations* for a complete list, including addresses. For example, the National Association of Female Executives, American Management Association, and American Association of University Women may have local chapters near your home. Check the Yellow Pages under "Associations." Professional groups (such as the Institute of Electrical Electronic Engineers, American Payroll Association, Professional Governmental Employees Association, American Dental Hygienist Association) offer education and career guidance information. Don't overlook associations; these are valuable resources in almost any field you may be interested in.

Another option in planning your future is to use the services of a qualified career counselor to help you map out a direction. He or she can help you develop a road map and a plan of action to succeed.

Another alternative is to go to a college and talk to an academic adviser. Community and technical colleges offer multitudes of training options to add to your skill set or completely change your career. Advisers and college placement officers can aid those investigating both four-year and graduate programs. Help is out there, so take advantage of it.

## Career Killer #5: Waiting for Employers

Too many frustrated clients have come to me because they did not get a promotion or raise, even though they had been doing a good job. In Debbie's case, she had finished her bachelor's degree, but no one had noticed. She was waiting for her employer to notice her and give her a raise or a promotion. Waiting . . . waiting . . . waiting. Nothing happened. She said, "I kept waiting for my boss to do something, waiting and expecting it should just *happen.*" Then Debbie changed. She went to personnel, got the job description for two other jobs in different departments, and rewrote her resumé. She applied. She got the call: Come down tomorrow for an interview. She spent those 24 hours creating her persuasion package. Those particular jobs did not appeal to her, so she kept at it. Within 45 days, the right position came along. Her qualifications weren't as strong as those of the two other candidates, but Debbie persuaded the hiring manager—and she got the job.

If you are waiting for your ship to come in, it's time to hoist your sails and steer your career to where you want to land.

## Career Killer #6: Lacking Self-Confidence

Self-limitations are the worst kind. They can prevent you from reaching new goals and enjoying new rewards. Believing "I can't do it," or "They'll never give me a raise," means you probably won't get it. Many of us lack the confidence to boldly demand more. But we can all *act* as if we possess confidence. You can act as if you merit a raise by outlining all your specific contributions to your employer. You can "act as if" you are the ideal candidate the employer can hire. The self-confidence you project doesn't have to be exactly what you feel inside. Many clients report they were calm on the outside but shaking in their boots on the inside. Yet they had researched their conversation and determined the correct approach, the important points to make. They came to the meeting armed with evidence of their achievements. Their persuasion package was ready, and they indeed achieved the goal: They got the raise, the new job, or the promotion they sought.

Janis was an accountant who'd left the workplace to start a family. She'd been out of the workforce for five years and was fearful no one would hire her with that big a work gap. Several interviews produced no job offers. Then she came to see me. I helped build her confidence that she would have a lot to offer an employer. When we went over her interviews and developed her persuasion package, the tools gave her even more confidence. (We had determined that she was too apologetic and sheepish in the interviews she'd had previously.) She felt better armed with the 5 Point Agenda and her 60 Second Sell (tools you'll learn about in Chapter 4). She sailed through the interview and told me, "I handled those salary questions just like you taught me. It worked—I got the job and more money than I ever dreamed I'd make."

Confidence and persuasion tools are essential elements to your long-term success.

## Career Killer #7: Letting *no* Stop You

Grace, a credit specialist for a large finance company, was heartbroken that a coworker got the promotion. Grace deserved it, wanted it, and had worked hard for it. She spoke to her boss, who encouraged her to wait. She did, and four months later another promotion went to someone else. She called me in tears. I empathized with her disappointment. We met a week later to review her situation. She had two choices—keep working and waiting or look for another job. She decided to investigate new options. Within 24 days she had sent out a dozen resumes—one for a customer service manager position she particularly wanted. She was called in for an interview. Her adrenaline was flowing. This was a management-level job—one she truly wanted. She worked hard to prepare for the interview. Grace faced a panel of eight for two hours. She convinced them. She got the job, moved into the higher ranks of management, and secured a $6,000 raise.

What can seem like total career derailment—being fired or passed over for promotion—often proves to be the exact motivator that drives you to something much, much better. Last year, 2,767,000 new jobs were created in America: You only need *one!*

## Career Killer #8: Money Is Everything

Liz was an excellent administrator. With ease, she could run a department, arrange a conference, and resolve a problem with a customer or employee. She was good at her job, and well paid. But administration was not her first love—training was. But few training jobs in her city would pay as well as her $70,000 administration position. Although Liz loved training others, her job called for only a small amount of it; still, she thrived on those opportunities. She studied learning patterns and was an active member in Toastmasters. As her managerial responsibilities increased, she always made time to present programs and to train. She developed a new employee training program. She led all the weekly sessions and relished the fun. Her boss was pleased with the program. He told her that they wanted her to take on more administrative responsibilities, so she was told to pass on her training duties to one of her staff. Liz pleaded against this change, but was overruled. That action by her boss made her decide that money meant very little if she was truly unhappy. It took a few months, but she landed a coveted job as a corporate trainer, accepting a salary of $43,000—a huge pay cut from the old job. Liz said she had a family meeting, and they all agreed to make some changes. Her family enjoys being around a happy Liz a lot more than the old miserable (richer) one. Liz learned a valuable life and career lesson: It's not worth it to slave at a job you hate, no matter how much it pays. When you love your work, it doesn't seem like work at all.

Satisfaction is the number one reason people elect to find to a new job. You will average 11,000 days at work over your lifetime. Choose the position that will make you feel happy, rewarded, and "lucky" you have such a great job to go to.

## Career Killer #9: Excuses

Getting fired, laid off, or losing out on a desired job or promotion can be a momentary setback: painful and disappointing, yes. Too often this rejection and pain can sabotage a person's future. You use the termination, your age, or lack of a degree to avoid getting back in the race and fighting harder for what you want.

I remember a client, Alan, who had been a successful sales rep at a Fortune 500 company. Politics and downsizing being what they were, he was forced into retirement at age 54. He seemed to lose his identity and eventually just got a job selling appliances at Sears. He told me he was "too old"; no one would hire him at his previous level. He felt hopeless, as two years had gone by since he "retired." We had three career coaching sessions and worked on his resumé and his job search action plan to target some potential companies. Then we developed his persuasion tools. I believed in Alan; his wife, kids, and friends had little hope for him. During each session we worked on his self-confidence and solid techniques he had not used or known of before. Two months after our sessions, he took a new position as an account rep with a growing company. In six months, he was the top salesperson, making over $100,000 in his first year with the company.

Excuses are just that—excuses that you, society, or others use to limit your success. Stop making them for yourself. No one can stop you but you. Never underestimate what you can achieve when you believe in yourself.

## You Define What Success Is for You

Success means different things to different people. Some people use a job title as a yardstick to determine success. Some tend to equate success with tangibles—income, the car they drive, the home and neighborhood they live in. Others view success in different terms—often finding fulfillment in helping others or caring for their family needs. Titles and career advancement can matter, too. For many of us, recognition seems to be a major component in our definition of success.

You can create whatever work situation will make you the happiest. For some, flexible hours and working from home is ideal. For others, a part-time job with extra leisure hours equals success. Still others aren't happy until they fill a VP spot. No one should impose their predetermined definition on you. Define success for yourself. Whatever makes you happy, whatever makes you perform at your best, whatever makes you have pride in your work contributions and enriches your life—that's what I call success.

## *Proven Strategies to Get What You Want*

Together, we are on a journey to achieve your dreams. *Your personal career satisfaction is the ultimate goal.* You may find you'll use this book at different stages in your career. Some chapters will be helpful when you want a new job. Others you'll consult when promotions and advancements are on your mind. Then again, there will come a time to check the guidelines on how to ask for a raise. Ultimately, you'll need to utilize the compensation strategies to negotiate a high starting salary or more benefits. Overall, there's a great deal of valuable guidance to help you better manage your career and navigate your future.

You'll find that this book teaches you proven tools, strategies, and communication techniques to achieve your goal.

As a career counselor for 18 years, I've worked with thousands of people to help them maximize their potential. My books are based on years of research, case studies, clients' experiences, plus my own expertise in hiring nearly 300 people and teaching employers' seminars on hiring. Every technique you'll learn has a proven track record of success.

I've used clients' stories (though the names have been changed for confidentiality reasons) to allow you to learn from real-life experiences: to be "inside" the performance review, to "hear" the salary negotiation. You'll get to "listen" to real conversations and gain important insights into what employers actually think. You'll learn what works and why. You'll also begin to develop your own formula for lifetime success and personal fulfillment—however you define those goals. Together, we'll solidify your *vision;* we'll then move on to the *action steps* needed to achieve your goals.

*Your success lies just ahead!*

# THE FUTURE AND YOUR SUCCESS

## LIVE EACH DAY TO THE FULLEST

*Live each day to the fullest. Get the most from each hour, each day, each age of your life. Then you can look forward with confidence, and back without regrets.*

*Be yourself—but be your best self. Dare to be different and to follow your own star.*

*And don't be afraid to be happy. Enjoy what is beautiful. Love with all your heart and soul. Believe that those you love, love you.*

*Forget what you have done for your friends, and remember what they have done for you. Disregard what the world owes you, and concentrate on what you owe the world.*

*When you are faced with a decision, make that decision as wisely as possible—then forget it. The moment of absolute certainty never arrives.*

*And above all, remember that God helps those who help themselves.*

*—ANONYMOUS*

The one factor that influences the workplace more than anything else is the impact that technology and the information age are having. Technology has revolutionized our jobs, forever changing the workplace and continually reshaping it. E-mail is a common tool in many large and small companies alike. "Virtual offices" have replaced real estate sites. Many regional managers and salespeople are equipped with computers, phones, faxes, and modems to operate from their homes, in hotels, or even in their cars. Technology is changing our offices, the tasks we do in our jobs, and how we perform them.

Living in the Seattle area, I've watched a company grow in just *one decade* from a small fledgling into a billion-dollar business operation. Most people would easily agree, Microsoft's tremendous growth and ability to seize the market opportunity has been nothing short of phenomenal. Bill Gates is a visionary and a marketing genius. And yet perhaps his greatest skill has been in recruiting hardworking, driven people who are

**CAREER COACH** *info*

**Flexibility and the willingness to learn new skills and apply these to the ever-changing job duties are essentials for succeeding in tomorrow's workplace.**

**CAREER COACH** *fact*

**Computer skills are the #1 skill employers want.**

committed to excelling at their jobs. These workers are dedicated to increasing the ease with which we can obtain, process, and use information. This major business transformation is shaping all of our lives, both at work and at home.

Technology requires increasingly advanced skills to operate and use equipment. Manufacturers have automated functions that once took 20 people, but now can be done with one sophisticated systems operator. It is the advances of technology that underlie one of the most important truths of career management.

Advancing your skill set and continuously adding to your arsenal will be a requirement to land the good jobs in the future. America has created millions of new jobs. The bad news is that many are low-paying service positions, such as retail clerks and food servers, where minimum wage is the norm. At the same time, high-paying management jobs have been eliminated. Middle managers, almost 9 million of them in 1990, have become victims of reorganizations and downsizing. As we enter the twenty-first century, it's predicted that only 3 million middle-management jobs will exist. Technology, with its proficient tracking systems, has allowed companies to increase the individual's productivity while garnering more people into self-directed work teams with one manager solely responsible for a large department—that is, no middle bosses between that manager and the workers.

Today, many employers won't consider workers who do not bring proficient computer skills (using programs such as Word and Excel) to the workplace.

The ability to retrieve, use, and communicate information has been transformed into e-mail messages, Internet research, team reports, newsletters, articles, even new policy and procedures. The information age dictates that we improve our written skills and verbal communications to give clear directions and keep people informed. Employers recognize, notice, actively recruit, and promote employees who have solid communications ability. With more emphasis on teamwork, interpersonal skills to get along with others is mandatory. Specifically, in a world where the boss says, "Research the Internet, download the important facts, write up a summary report, e-mail it, and then present it to the team," most are finding computer skills are imperative to do the job.

Technology is and will remain the most major impact influencing the workplace in the years to come.

**Employers hire people who add value to the organization.**

## New Hiring Methodology

Employers are expanding the old method of "find some-one who fills the job description" to a broader concept in their hiring practices. Large companies and small are seeking a set of job skills that includes the ability to perform at a higher level of productivity and to interact in a positive manner to get the work done. The work will evolve and change—many times by your own suggestion. People are tied more to skill sets, strengths, and flexibility to what's needed in today's marketplace than to a narrow job duties' description.

Potential bosses look for personal traits and standards of quality and excellence when reviewing your background. Personal productivity, including an attitude toward success, is a new measuring stick to evaluate potential employees. Microsoft has long been known as an employer that demands the very best from employees. Although the company has a 40-hour workweek, employees normally average 70 hours a week. High pressure, stemming from employees' internal desire to do their very best and whatever it takes to get the job done, is the common operating procedure on Microsoft's campus. Nearly 20,000 people put forth that kind of effort every day. They are excited about their jobs, their work, and are ecstatic about their company and the products it produces.

Over 120,000 resumés were sent to Microsoft's personnel office last year—evidence that this is a coveted place many wish to work at. Although the intensity and hours may be unsettling to you, they are not intimidating to those who choose to work there. They have a passion for their own personal excellence and achievement. It pushes them to be more creative, try new things, learn more, and do it better. It's a personal philosophy I've lived my life by. My goal is to help people find better jobs. I devote endless hours to this pursuit. It's not "work" to me, but my life passion and mission. I spend days and nights endeavoring to make it easier and faster for you to land a job. I hardly notice that my typical work week usually exceeds 70 hours.

*Develop your own personal excellence formula.* It takes such a small amount of effort to move from being an average worker to being a good worker in an employer's eyes. When you team your passionate performance attitude, your specific skills, and your willingness to acquire new abilities, you have the formula for lifelong career success and satisfaction.

## Real-Life Choices

*Choices.* Everybody has them and everybody makes them. My most memorable career decision was a painful one. I'd grown very unhappy with the dysfunctional politics in my department at the university. I distinctly remember driving home, tears streaming down my face at another frustrating encounter with a difficult (and "unfireable") employee who hated her job and made everyone miserable. At that moment, I decided to quit. After following through with that decision, I started my own company. My vision to help people find jobs and the freedom to choose my own path have made me happy and extremely satisfied in the career choice I've made.

*Choices.* Martha and Natalie worked in the personnel office of a prominent retailer. Martha was the human resources director, and Natalie, the training director. Both had been there over 10 years. Natalie became dissatisfied and discouraged with the company's lack of innovation and progressiveness. As she finished her master's degree, she expanded her network and job search to land a coveted training position with the Ritz Carleton's corporate office. Martha, the HR manager, on the other hand, found it easier to tolerate the negative status quo. She viewed the job as a paycheck and denied that her company's internal and financial problems were as severe as they were. Eighteen months after Natalie had moved on, Martha lost her job, as the company's bankruptcy closed the doors. Two years later she had not gotten a new position and put little hope in finding a new job. Both women saw the "writing on the wall." Their individual choices—and thus their outcomes—were very different.

*Choices.* No one was more devastated at the loss of his Cancer Society regional director's job than Kevin. Without a degree, he'd moved up the ranks to regional executive director. Cost cutting ended his job. For eight months, nothing happened. Friends blamed his age (over 40) or lack of a college degree as the culprit. They were wrong. When Kevin came to me for career counseling, our first objective was to focus him on success and create an action plan. I told him he had to make a choice: a choice to succeed, and thus do everything it took to reach the goal of a new job. Or he

**Today's workers must develop a strong sense of loyalty to themselves first and their company second.**

could choose to fail by blaming others. He took the challenge, and within a few weeks, with renewed effort and by using more successful search methods, he landed a new job. He wrote to say, "It's been a huge learning experience, and I intend to finish my college degree and never take my career for granted again. I know I made some poor assumptions. This time I learned how to really find a good job. Now I know I can obtain whatever I go after and am willing to work hard for." *Choices.*

Job or career problems are opportunities in disguise. You may not like the choices at first—layoffs, firings, bad bosses—all can be difficult to deal with. But you *can* change yourself and your future for the better. You need to look more closely at *who you are* and *what you value;* then decide specifically what you want and how to achieve it. We all have choices—choices to create a better and more satisfying place for ourselves.

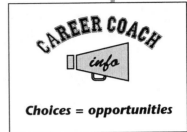

**Choices = opportunities**

**The only constant in the workplace is that it is continuously changing.**

## *Survival Tools for Career Success*

There are specifics that you'll need to advance in the world of tomorrow. Personal traits, education, work expertise will all become your "portable career"—a career that moves with you from one employer to another. Persuasion skills (the ability to convince employers) are also essential to your career management.

Here are some of the major trends, guidelines, and changes that you'll need to understand as you select the road and paths your career will follow.

### Career Trends

✔ The average worker will experience over 10 job changes during his or her lifetime.

✔ Job security lies in your ability to land a new job.

✔ Personal accountability on the job will continue to increase.

✔ You will be given more power and autonomy to perform your work.

✔ New advancement opportunities will continue to open up for women and minorities.

✔ An employer's demand for your time and productivity will continue to increase.

✔ More advanced technology will be introduced into the workplace.

✔ Skills and educational training will be a job requirement.

✔ More jobs will define themselves.

✔ With fewer opportunities to advance, more moves will be lateral.

✔ Change will be the one constant in the workplace.

✔ Increased importance will continue to be placed on the organization's bottom line.

✔ Companies will seek added value from employees.

✔ Small companies will create two-thirds of all new jobs.

✔ A global economy will dictate the need for competitive products as it influences job creation and work demands.

✔ Employees will move to the geographical locations where the jobs are.

✔ There are always good jobs open, available, and actively being recruited for, no matter what the economy is.

## Personal Guidelines

✔ Develop a skill set—skills, talents, and experiences.

✔ Adopt attitudes that focus on personal excellence and quality.

✔ Be highly productive, organized, and efficient.

✔ Continuously acquire new skills.

✔ Emphasize customer service, whether your customers are internal departments or external clients.

✔ Work well in a team.

✔ Focus your time and energy on success and successful pursuits.

✔ Reward yourself for both small and big jobs well done.

✔ Celebrate your victories.

✔ Put your personal goals and well-being ahead of company loyalty.

✔ Develop a reputation for integrity, fairness, and honesty.

✔ Continuously develop your professional network.

✔ Be involved in professional organizations/associations within your field.

✔ Remain current in your field.

✔ Do more than expected, and do it better than expected.

## Self-Marketing Strategies

✔ Review your career every year and map out an annual plan.

✔ Do quality work in a productive manner.

✔ Perfect your persuasion skills.

✔ Acquire solid references attesting to past performance and excellence.

✔ Believe in yourself.

✔ Have a current, up-to-date resumé ready.

✔ Pay attention to potential career opportunities.

✔ Obtain the needed education and skills to land the jobs you want.

You design your future by the choices you make. You can reshape your world for the better, or watch it turn dim and bleak. Remember, as life deals its cards, you *always* have options. Take control of your own destiny. The future is what you make it.

# DEFINE YOUR BEST SKILLS AND IDEAL JOB

## HAPPINESS

*The road to happiness lies in two simple principles: find what it is that interests you and that you can do well, and when you find it put your whole soul into it—every bit of energy and ambition and natural ability you have.*

—*JOHN D. ROCKEFELLER*

The biggest mistake many people make is not having a clear vision that targets a specific job. This vision is essential and necessary. Once you know the position you desire, you can analyze the skills needed to perform the job. Then you can begin to create your persuasion package to obtain the job. You can manage your career to move in a progressive path all the way up to CEO if that's what you desire and are willing to work for.

Career satisfaction is a result of aligning your skills, your values, and your interest. Too often, people want to skip over the career and skill assessment part; they don't wish to spend the time on this self-analysis. Don't do it. Skipping this chapter is a mistake. You'll quickly define some very specific skills that you can offer an employer as you finish these exercises. The key to getting hired is to focus on telling potential employers how you can fill their needs and do the job they want done. The skill identification will be very helpful in allowing you to assess the multiple talents you possess. Then you'll narrow down the organization—the type, field, interest, size—that's ideal for you. Once you complete this chapter, you'll be ready to talk to employers, having defined your strongest, most marketable skills.

The "318 Skills You Could Offer an Employer" list is an easy way to identify your acquired skills. Be complete and thorough as you proceed through this list. You will be amazed by the number of skills you possess and can sell to an employer.

The "Values Grid" allows you to consider which aspects of work are the most important. It provides you with a framework to guide your decisions as you investigate companies and various jobs. Your priorities change over your lifetime. What's important at age 25—a good salary and progressive company—might get replaced at age 49 by a strong desire to give back to the community by helping others. Values influence and shape your career decisions and are an important motivator in your career planning and job selection.

The "Interest List" is significant to bring pleasure to your work. If you love computers, working at a software company will allow you to be with others who share your passion. If you love sports, you might find working for a pro team ideal, even if you can't play for them. If you love parties, an event planner might be the perfect job. If care for others defines your goals, a hospital setting or healthcare provider might be a good choice for you. Examine both personal and professional interests. Let your thoughts roam, and record everything that comes to mind—movies, travel, family—anything you enjoy hearing about or doing.

The next charts record association, community, or civic work you may have been involved with. Many times, these are the places where you have the opportunity to try out and hone new skills. Many leaders got their first exposure to management in these nonpaid positions.

Honors, awards, and positions of leadership add to the overall picture. You can note meetings chaired and offices held as well. Include both volunteer and employer-related experiences.

The last section involves identifying your ideal job and the company profile that most appeals to you. Once you've progressed to the end of this you should have a much clearer idea of both the job title and company you seek.

Let's start your career assessment with the "318 Skills You Could Offer an Employer" list. Check every skill you possess. This is an excellent tool to count up all the good things you've got going for you. Then proceed onto the other exercises.

# 318 Skills You Could Offer an Employer

| Possess | Type of Skill |
|---|---|
| | Directing work flow |
| | Implementing decisions |
| | Enforcing regulations |
| | Multitasking |
| | Program administration |
| | Coordinating services |
| | Planning events |
| | Advising others |
| | Problem solving |
| | Compiling research data |
| | Analyzing data |
| | Conducting research |
| | Diagnosing problems |
| | Systematizing |
| | Organizing processes |
| | Organizing programs |
| | Organizing people |
| | Troubleshooting |
| | Investigating problems |
| | Offering evaluations on situations |
| | Ability to examine and evaluate complex data |
| | Proposing solutions or recommendations |
| | Mediating between groups |
| | Dealing creatively with colors, spaces, shapes, dimensions, ceramics, art |
| | Drawing or painting a picture or design |
| | Assessment of needs |
| | Budget management |
| | Preparing budgets |
| | Keeping financial records |
| | Developing financial forecasts/projections |
| | Running financial simulations |
| | Paying bills |
| | Authorizing checks/treasury responsibility |

| Possess | Type of Skill |
|---|---|
| | **Communications skills:** |
| | **Verbally exchanging information in a clear understandable manner** |
| | **Written skills that effectively communicate in correspondences** |
| | **Writing proposals** |
| | **COMPUTER SKILLS** |
| | **Platforms:** |
| | **PC** |
| | **Macintosh** |
| | **Network-specific hardware:** |
| | **Operating systems:** |
| | **DOS** |
| | **Windows** |
| | **Programming languages:** |
| | **Software:** |
| | **Word** |
| | **Excel** |
| | **WordPerfect** |
| | **Lotus** |
| | **PageMaker** |
| | **Others:** |
| | **Systems analysis:** |
| | **Hardware/troubleshooting** |
| | **Network programming ability** |
| | **Ability to train others on computer usage** |
| | **Providing technical support** |
| | **Ability to point out and rectify errors in a positive manner** |
| | **Counseling others through the sharing of ideas, opinions, advice, guidance, or emotional support** |
| | **Coaching others toward improved behavior or performance** |
| | **Ability to develop new ideas or processes** |
| | **Highly imaginative with many innovative ideas** |
| | **Ability to translate ideas into written or visual form for others** |
| | **Highly creative in applying theory to develop or design new things** |

| Possess | Type of Skill |
|---|---|
| | Producing new products or programs |
| | Designing flyers, brochures, booklets, etc. |
| | Inventing new products |
| | Designing marketing materials |
| | Developing marketing campaign |
| | Classifying and recording data/information |
| | Delegating tasks to others |
| | Developing ideas from the thought concept through to completion |
| | Documenting records |
| | Filing records |
| | Setting realistic objectives for self and others |
| | Ability to determine a goal or goals to be worked toward |
| | Visionary |
| | Establishing priorities by sorting tasks according to order of importance and/or urgency |
| | Ability to appraise or determine the quality of, the worth of, and/or the effectiveness of a program or organization |
| | Ability to evaluate a person's performance |
| | Ability to direct or lead the way to a particular goal or objective |
| | Implementation to bring an idea or plan into reality |
| | Improving a condition, situation, product, or process |
| | Ability to influence the thoughts and actions of others and get results |
| | Ability to examine a piece of work carefully and detect flaws or errors |
| | Speaking, writing, understanding another language |
| | Interpreting and translating a different language |
| | Public speaking |
| | Instructing or teaching others |
| | Editing written words |
| | Writing—articles, publications, newsletters |
| | Authoring a book |
| | Training to perform a task |
| | Debating an issue |
| | Leading an organization |
| | Leading a project |

| Possess | Type of Skill |
|---|---|
| | Leading a department |
| | Organizing work flow for others |
| | Taking risks |
| | Managing people |
| | Project management |
| | Directing or guiding a group by assigning specific duties and maintaining harmonious relations |
| | Ability to acquire knowledge of a subject or obtaining a skill by study, experience, and/or instruction |
| | Effectively hearing what the speaker is attempting to communicate |
| | Using active listening skills to draw people out and help them express their thoughts |
| | Managing people and being responsible for them and their work |
| | Helping build a team through recognizing, directing, and utilizing the skills of others |
| | Directing the process, resources, coordination, and work to achieve desired results |
| | Constructing or assembling things |
| | Operating equipment or machinery |
| | Fixing or repairing equipment |
| | Data entry |
| | Money management |
| | Developing and maintaining financial tracking systems |
| | Ability to motivate and inspire others to perform at higher levels |
| | Negotiation skills to arrive jointly at decisions, conclusions or, solutions |
| | Ability to exchange ideas, information, and opinions with others to formulate policies and programs |
| | Accounting or bookkeeping |
| | Doing cost analysis |
| | Calculating/counting/taking inventory |
| | Purchasing products or services |
| | Conducting statistical analysis |
| | Organizing processes or systems |
| | Planning and coordinating meetings or special events |
| | Performing or acting |

| Possess | Type of Skill |
|---------|---------------|
| | **Playing music** |
| | **Composing music** |
| | **Making people laugh** |
| | **Singing** |
| | **Making presentations** |
| | **Ability to influence attitudes and ideas of others in favor of a desired point of view** |
| | **Selling products or services** |
| | **Ability to modify or adapt behavior** |
| | **Promoting events** |
| | **Influencing others** |
| | **Promoting products or services** |
| | **Corporate promotions** |
| | **Persuading others** |
| | **Strategic planning** |
| | **System planning** |
| | **Planning large-scale projects or designs** |
| | **Process improvement through the examination, streamlining, development, or design of more efficient or effective ways to perform a task or function** |
| | **Ability to design and outline the framework of a new program** |
| | **Program development to enhance or improve an existing program** |
| | **Ability to bring a program or plan into existence** |
| | **Ability to interest others in and/or sell ideas, goods, programs, projects, or services** |
| | **Policymaking** |
| | **Visualizing and balancing factors** |
| | **Global thinking** |
| | **Ability to recruit new employees, membership, subscribers, etc.** |
| | **Ability to refer or direct people to appropriate sources of aid and/or information** |
| | **Ability to prepare either a formal or informal report describing the results of a particular occurrence** |
| | **Ability to serve as an agent or representative for others authorized to work and speak on their behalf to accomplish desired results** |

| Possess | Type of Skill |
| --- | --- |
| | Ability to undertake careful, original, systematic study, research, and investigation in some field of knowledge to discover or establish facts or principles |
| | Applying what others have developed |
| | Demonstrating follow-through |
| | Being a detail-orientated person |
| | Focusing on project, task, or problem at hand |
| | Scheduling others |
| | Ability to prepare a coordinated, timed plan for procedure on a project, which entails making arrangements for events and processes as well as making sure goals or promises are delivered on time |
| | Ability to choose between various products, services, or people by using certain standards of excellence or quality |
| | Self-motivating: possessing an inner drive that causes or directs working toward a particular goal or moving in a particular direction |
| | Helping to build or improve the quality of a staff through training, counseling, guidance, and goal objectives |
| | Ability to summarize and make a brief, concise statement presenting the substance or general idea or main points of a subject |
| | Ability to determine or interpret work procedures for a group of workers |
| | Assigning specific duties to workers and supervising those actions |
| | Promoting efficiency in others |
| | Ability to motivate workers |
| | Building a cohesive, highly productive team that meets goals on time |
| | Ability to give instructions or lessons enabling others to learn (via explanation, demonstration, and/or supervised practice) |
| | Observing others |
| | Examining products or processes |
| | Inspecting products |
| | Diagnosing problems |
| | Showing attention to details |
| | Bringing enthusiasm and energy into group |
| | Demonstrating strong interpersonal skills |

| Possess | Type of Skill |
|---------|---------------|
| | Calculating numerical data |
| | Collecting money |
| | Negotiating contracts |
| | Coordinating events |
| | Designing ads/products |
| | Investigating problems |
| | Handling complaints |
| | Inspecting physical objects |
| | Operating equipment |
| | Planning agendas |
| | Interviewing others |
| | Fundraising |
| | Rehabilitating others |
| | Repairing mechanical devices |
| | Facilitating meetings |
| | Drawing charts |
| | Creating graphs |
| | Producing publications |
| | Updating files |
| | Handling community relations |
| | Providing community services |
| | Handling contracts and agreements |
| | Curriculum development |
| | Providing customer service |
| | Decorating interiors |
| | Designing buildings |
| | Creating displays |
| | Drafting |
| | Producing films or videos |
| | Providing financial analysis |
| | Financial planning |
| | Hiring employees |
| | Evaluating inventory control |
| | Conducting market research |
| | Handling product merchandising |
| | Using multimedia equipment |

| Possess | Type of Skill |
|---|---|
| | Creating multimedia products, presentations, or designs |
| | Printing project coordination |
| | Copywriting |
| | Quality assurance |
| | Quality improvement |
| | Testing others |
| | Word-processing skills |
| | Conceptualizing ideas |
| | Acting as liaison, go-between, or intermediary |
| | Adapting to changing situations and needs |
| | Adapting tools, machinery, and equipment |
| | Adjusting, arranging, or adapting information |
| | Redesigning tools or equipment |
| | Allocating or dispensing resources |
| | Assembling or collecting materials |
| | Assessing a person's performance using equipment |
| | Assessing the performance of equipment |
| | Auditing or balancing financial information |
| | Budgeting time, resources, or materials |
| | Building things with tools and equipment |
| | Collaborating with others on a project |
| | Collating or sorting objects, materials, or papers |
| | Comparing objects |
| | Completing projects or tasks on schedule |
| | Controling costs |
| | Coping with deadlines and time pressure |
| | Coping with difficulties |
| | Critiquing or reviewing others' work |
| | Demonstrating how to do things |
| | Detecting problems or errors |
| | Developing prototypes |
| | Dispensing medicines |
| | Drafting or drawing inanimate objects |
| | Editing written material |
| | Establishing policy or procedures |
| | Estimating cost, distance, size, etc. |

| Possess | Type of Skill |
|---------|---------------|
|  | Executing, implementing, getting something done |
|  | Expediting, speeding things along |
|  | Filling orders or requests |
|  | Following through on tasks |
|  | Terminating employees |
|  | Identifying and seizing opportunities |
|  | Illustrating or depicting products |
|  | Improving tools, machines, or equipment |
|  | Improvising |
|  | Indexing or organizing data or information |
|  | Informing or giving out information to others |
|  | Installing equipment |
|  | Justifying decisions or conclusions |
|  | Keeping secrets or confidential information |
|  | Performing lab work |
|  | Listening perceptively |
|  | Making contacts and bringing people together |
|  | Making layouts |
|  | Making models |
|  | Possessing manual dexterity, eye-hand coordination |
|  | Measuring boundaries, sizes, or weights |
|  | Mentoring others |
|  | Merging or combining ideas or systems |
|  | Mobilizing resources and people |
|  | Monitoring machines, equipment, processes |
|  | Observing and monitoring data, people, or things |
|  | Ordering supplies |
|  | Originating new ideas or procedures |
|  | Perceiving needs of others |
|  | Proofreading |
|  | Interviewing people |
|  | Creating advertising materials |
|  | Reading and using reference materials |
|  | Reconciling financial records |
|  | Regulating things |
|  | Rehabilitating people |

| Possess | Type of Skill |
|---------|---------------|
| | Screening applicants |
| | Selecting items or products |
| | Setting criteria or standards of quality |
| | Setting up systems, services, or programs |
| | Surveying for information or opinions |
| | Surveying land |
| | Systematizing |
| | Tabulating information or data |
| | Taking accurate measurements |
| | Tolerating interruptions, inconveniences |
| | Handling routine or boring tasks |
| | Tutoring others |
| | Using sophisticated equipment, instruments |
| | Using personal contacts, networks |
| | Visualizing ideas or future trends |
| | Working with animals |
| | Writing technical materials |
| | Appraising property |
| | Approving layouts or designs |
| | Committee work |
| | Constructing buildings or other things |
| | Credit analysis |
| | Interior decorating |
| | Estimating space or cost requirements |
| | Expediting process |
| | Legal expertise |
| | Making business deals |
| | Merchandising of product(s) |
| | Painting objects |
| | Reducing costs |
| | Understanding technical manuals, terminology |
| | Setting up demonstrations (shows, exhibits, displays) |
| | Supervising installations |
| | Supervising staff |
| | Supervising construction projects |

| Possess | Type of Skill |
|---------|---------------|
|         | Time management |
|         | Treating ill people |
|         | Using scientific/medical instruments |

List any additional specialty skills or industry knowledge important and marketable for the new job you seek:

I have the ability to speak & conversate with anyone

You possess more skills than you ever imagined—skills employers want and will pay you for. Now let's consolidate the results a bit. Select your top 10 skills. Choose those you are proficient at and also enjoy using.

MY TOP 10 SKILLS

1. Dealing creatively w/ colors
2. Advising others
3. ability to examine a piece of work
4. Selling products & services & detect flaws or errors
5. Visualizing & balancing factors
6. Scheduling others
7. Observing others
8. creating displays
9. Improvising
10. working with animals

Now let's move on and complete the rest of your self-assessment.

# *Values Assessment*

## HOW IMPORTANT ARE THESE WORK VALUES TO YOU?

| | Unimportant | Somewhat Important | Moderately Important | Very Important |
|---|---|---|---|---|
| Salary | | | X | |
| Status and prestige | | | X | |
| Travel opportunities | X | | | |
| Leisure time | | | | X |
| Power and influence | | X | | |
| Competition | | X | | |
| Being around interesting people | | | X | |
| Blending of family and career | | | X | |
| Variety and change in work | | | | X |
| Involvement in decision making | | | X | |
| Security | | | X | |
| Public contact | X | | | |
| Recognition | | | | X |
| Flexible work schedule | | | | X |
| Regular 40-hour workweek | | | X | |
| Challenging work | | | X | |
| Independence | | | | X |
| Benefits | | X | | |
| Quality of product | | | X | |
| Freedom from pressure/stress | | | X | |
| Opportunities for advancement | | | | X |
| Clear rules and expectations | | | | X |
| Autonomy in job | | X | | |
| Friendships at work | | | X | |
| Helping others | | X | | |
| Creativity | | | | X |
| Beautiful work surroundings | | | X | |
| Acquiring new knowledge | | | | X |
| Taking risks | | | X | |
| Supervising others | | X | | |
| Working with a team | | | | X |
| Working alone | | | | X |
| Working with details | | | | X |

# 50 Interests

**LIST BOTH PERSONAL AND PROFESSIONAL INTERESTS**

animal husbandry

outdoor activity

drawing

painting

conversating

yoga

romance

beauty

family

travel

woring in a professional

organization atmospher

clean

nowing clientelle

communication

design

creating

# *Association/Community/Civic Activities*

| Date | List activity |
|------|---------------|
|      |               |
|      |               |
|      |               |
|      |               |
|      |               |
|      |               |
|      |               |
|      |               |

## Awards Received

| Date | List award |
|------|------------|
|      | Best / gemstone training |
|      | macys / shopped ? |
|      |            |
|      |            |
|      |            |
|      |            |
|      |            |

## Honors Bestowed

| Date | List award |
|------|------------|
|      |            |
|      |            |
|      |            |
|      |            |
|      |            |
|      |            |
|      |            |

## Positions of Leadership Held

| Date(s) | List position |
|---------|---------------|
|         |               |
|         |               |
|         |               |
|         |               |
|         |               |
|         |               |
|         |               |
|         |               |

We now need to consolidate and sift through this information you've just completed. Prioritization forces you to make choices and decisions about yourself and your goals. This will determine your professional profile.

# *Professional Profile*

**MY TOP 10 PREVIOUS JOB SKILLS ARE:**

1. _____

2. _____

3. _____

4. _____

5. _____

6. _____

7. _____

8. _____

9. _____

10. _____

**MY TOP FIVE *INTERESTS* ARE:**

1. _____

2. _____

3. _____

4. _____

5. _____

**MY TOP FIVE *VALUES* ARE:**

1. _____

2. _____

3. _____

4. _____

5. _____

# *Defining the Ideal Job*

## Company Profile

Visualize the exact type of company you want to work for. Select the environment that will make you feel good and will encourage your productivity.

**TYPE OF ORGANIZATION**
**Check Those That Apply, Then Select One Ideal**

|  |  |
|---|---|
|  | Small (100 or less employers) |
|  | Midsize (101–1,000 employees) |
|  | Medium (1,001–5,000 employees) |
|  | Large (5,001–10,000 employees) |
|  | Major (over 10,000 employees) |
|  | Your own company |
|  |  |
|  | Corporation |
|  | Federal or state government |
|  | County or city/town government |
|  | Nonprofit |

## INDUSTRY TYPE
### Check Those That Apply

|  | High growth |
|---|---|
|  | Stable |
|  | Turnaround |
|  | Prestigious |
|  | Industry leader |
|  | Slower pace |

## PREFERRED INDUSTRY
### Check Those That Apply

|  | High tech |
|---|---|
|  | Telecommunications |
|  | Education |
|  | Retail |
|  | Service |
|  | Manufacturing |
|  | Business |
|  | Hospitality |
|  | Tourism |
|  | Healthcare |
|  | Education |
|  | Construction |

## SALARY DESIRED
### Check One

|  | Less than $25,000 |
|---|---|
|  | $25,000–30,000 |
|  | $31,000–$35,000 |
|  | $36,000–$40,000 |
|  | $41,000–$45,000 |
|  | $46,000–$50,000 |
|  | $51,000–$55,000 |
|  | $56,000–$60,000 |
|  | $61,000–$70,000 |
|  | $71,000–$80,000 |
|  | $81,000–$90,000 |
|  | $91,000–$100,000 |
|  | Over $100,000 |

## BENEFITS DESIRED
**Rank in Order of Importance/Priority—Select Only 1 through 5**

| | |
|---|---|
| | Not important |
| | Medical |
| | Dental |
| | Vision |
| | Retirement plan |
| | Profit sharing |
| | Establishment |
| | Bonus structure |
| | Commissions |
| | Maternity/paternity leave |
| | Flextime |
| | Vacations: |
| | 1 week |
| | 2 weeks |
| | 3 weeks |
| | 4 weeks |
| | More |

## GEOGRAPHIC LOCATION
**Check One**

| | |
|---|---|
| | Will not relocate |
| | Desired new location: _____ |
| | Potential job openings in area: _____ |
| | Potential employers: _____ |

## MANAGEMENT LEVEL
**That You Desire to Hold in Your Next Job**

| | |
|---|---|
| | Nonmanagement |
| | Professional—no supervising responsibilities |
| | Work in team |
| | Team leader |
| | Manage up to _____ employees |
| | Work primarily independently of others |
| | Department head |
| | Division head |

| | |
|---|---|
| | Product/service manager |
| | Vice president |
| | Senior executive (title: _____ ) |
| | CEO |
| | Other: |

## EDUCATION
### Check Those That Apply, Fill in Respectively

| | Degree Conferred | Major | College Name | Year |
|---|---|---|---|---|
| | Doctorate | | | |
| | Master's degree | | | |
| | Bachelor's degree | | | |
| | Associate's degree | | | |

## SPECIAL CREDENTIALS

| Date | List designations (MBA, JD, CPA, PE, etc.) |
|---|---|
| | |
| | |
| | |
| | |
| | |

Now, take the time to define the perfect job. You've examined your background, skills, education, and you've identified the specific job title you seek. After reviewing the following sample, write out and define the particulars that would make a job ideal for you.

## SAMPLE IDEAL JOB

### Job Title: Product Marketing Manager

My ideal company is medium in size, but really an emerging high-tech company. I'm head of a new product marketing campaign. I'm overseeing 100 employees in this process. The work is challenging, exciting, high pressure. Salary is $80,000, with a major bonus tied to product success. I hold an MBA and am computer-proficient in both Excel and Word. My strongest skills are planning, budget management, coordination, interpersonal relations, and problem solving.

**YOUR IDEAL JOB**

**Job Title:** _____

**Description:** _____

_____

_____

_____

_____

_____

_____

_____

_____

_____

_____

_____

_____

_____

_____

_____

_____

_____

_____

_____

## *Resources When You Need More Career Guidance*

It makes sense to take the time to do thorough self-analysis. Your happiness depends on it. A good career counselor can clearly point out options you've overlooked. Their expertise is to analyze the world of work, then direct you to new options as they assess your talents and skills. Many community colleges offer career counseling at no charge, but with limited or restricted services. Most major cities have career counselors listed in the Yellow Pages under "Vocational Guidance" or "Career Counseling."

## Career Counseling

### TO FIND A QUALIFIED CAREER COUNSELOR

✔ Ask for referrals from friends, and check with college career centers in your area.

✔ Obtain the counselor's marketing brochure and fees.

✔ Investigate the counselor's qualifications. Reputable counselors have a college degree (preferably a master's or higher) with vocational counseling emphasis.

✔ Comparison shop. Training and experience vary greatly.

✔ Use counselors with a well-established reputation that charge an hourly fee. Avoid organizations that sell $3,000 (or higher) packages to help you find a job. Too many of these packaged programs use fear and intimidation as sales practices to get your money, but never live up to the promise that they'll find you a job. (The small print has an escape clause that doesn't guarantee you anything.) A recent article in *Money* magazine identified these high-priced packages as the number one consumer rip-off in America.

✔ Select a counselor whose style is a good fit for you and your needs. Some counselors specialize in the self-analysis and career exploration phase. Others may have more expertise in the job search process—writing resumés, cover letters, targeting companies, and helping prepare for interviews. You may need to use more than one counselor to aid you in achieving your goals.

## Vocational Testing

Most community colleges offer vocational testing to the general public. However, many people expect to take a test and get a definitive answer. There is *no test* you can take that will tell you 30 minutes later exactly what you should be. Typically, you invest hundreds of dollars to take a battery of tests. Two commonly given are the Strong Campbell Interest Inventory and the Myers-Briggs Type Indicator. Tests are simply a piece of the puzzle—one component of your decision on career choices. I've found numerous other factors may limit your choice of career: desire, time, money, family situation, and whether you are willing to obtain the necessary training, degrees, or even to relocate. If you really want to uncover your talents to direct yourself to a new career, you must combine the testing with a good counselor who will interpret the results and help direct you.

I've had extensive experience with most testing instruments, and I've found one resource to be the better option: I recommend the Johnson O'Connor Research Foundation, a nonprofit vocational testing service, which has 11 offices across the country that offer its three-day testing program. (Call the Foundation's main office at 800-355-3672 for more details.)

# *Future Possibilities*

Once you've compiled all the information, I recommend you stop and do some research on your field and chosen job target. You need to be exact as to the training and skills necessary to move into your next position. Ask yourself the hard questions: What do I need to add to my skills set to move on? A new degree? Specialized training? A specific new skill? The future can hold many options, so we must identify both our long-term and short-term goals. Let's consider your options.

## Is the Grass Any Greener?

Whitney had been with her nonprofit employer for eight years. The job had grown and expanded. She was a department head, liked her job, but admitted to me that it had gotten pretty routine. She came to see me because a friend had encouraged her to apply for a director position that was open. We worked on her resumé and cover letter. Whitney was tremendously excited about the new possibility. The salary would be higher, and it would be a promotion to move into a new position as a director. The next week flew by, and Whitney was called in for an interview. We had another session where we worked on her persuasion package. She went in armed with her 60 Second Sell and 5 Point Agenda—communication tools you'll learn how to create in Chapter 4. The interview went exceptionally well. Whitney did an excellent job marketing herself. She called me to say that she had a panel interview in front of five people; it was stressful, but she felt it went well. Three days later, Whitney was called by Steve, the departing director, who had not been involved in the selection committee. He was a man she knew only slightly, but he was well admired. The conversation he had with Whitney was quite disturbing. They met at a restaurant, where he shared with her exactly why he was leaving the association. It seemed that two women managers were in a constant battle over the last year. Both had applied for the director job and neither would get it. He hinted that Whitney was the top choice. He said that the strain of the politics and the draining conflict between the two managers had become unbearable. They sabotaged each other and often went over his head to the board. He admitted he'd lost total control. Since the board refused to fire these managers, his life had turned into a management nightmare. He said he wanted her to know the actual picture so she could make a more informed choice when she was offered the position. He left with the warning that both women would be resentful of anyone who got the director position. Each one felt she should have gotten the job offer.

Whitney returned to her office and saw a message from the chairman of the selection committee. Sure enough, they offered her the job. They felt she was the ideal person to move them forward and increase both membership and revenues with her innovative ideas and leadership. She had thought this was her dream job; and it was, until about two hours ago. She called me for advice and decided to trust her boss, John, who was a close colleague of the departing director. She went to his office, where John closed the door and listened to Whitney explain her situation. He told her that it was a pretty dysfunctional office and that Steve, the current director, was burned out by the staff conflict. Her boss felt the situation and conflict would surely continue. John's assessment was grim. He did inquire why she had applied. Whitney confessed that the chance to be sole director and the salary were the primary lures. He nodded and said: "The choice is yours. Choose carefully."

At five o'clock, Whitney called and turned down the job. She knew that the energy needed to bring out change and improvements would be impossible with such a staff conflict interfering at every turn. She felt disappointed that the "dream job" had disintegrated. As we discussed her decision, I kept pointing out that perhaps she was already in her "dream job." She liked the boss, her coworkers, and their association's members. She'd built a good team, and John, her boss, was always open to new ideas. She became rejuvenated and began to plot a new course where she was. Three months later, Whitney met with John to discuss a promotion. The following week, she moved into a new position as assistant director. She admitted to me that the grass was not greener in the sought-after director's job, but she was glad that she looked. As a result, she changed. She breathed new life into the job she had and renewed her energy and enthusiasm there. She plotted it out and went to John with a well-developed plan to finalize the new job as assistant director that had been discussed but not acted upon. She drew up a budget that would allow her to receive additional compensation and realign her staff and duties without requiring additional outside funds. It turned out well for her, and Whitney said she couldn't be happier.

Rick was an ambitious man, both smart and aggressive. He'd spent his 18-year career in the pharmacy area at the city's most prominent hospital. During that time, he'd earned an MBA and had advanced to become the assistant director. He was thrilled the day that the top job, director of pharmacy, became available. It was a coveted position, and several managers inside the hospital wanted it. It was a tough job, too, as the hospital was in the midst of a major restructuring process that would surely result in layoffs and downsizing. In fact, ten top department heads had recently been let go. Competition was keen. Besides internal applicants, 200 outside candidates applied. Eight people, one of whom was Rick, got interviews. He prepared and felt he'd done his best at the interview. Rick acknowledged, though, that the office politics were at an all-time high. He did not get the job; instead, someone from outside landed the only job he really wanted. He was severely disappointed and discouraged. Choices: to stay or go? Would the grass be greener elsewhere? Rick had done some consulting on the side but had no other job options. He was angry and upset to be passed by. We met and discussed his situation. He had three options: (1) remain in the status quo job with no possibility of promotion, (2) quit and consult, or (3) wait until he found another job.

Middle-management jobs across the country were quickly being eliminated. Rick realized that the trend toward downsizing would make finding another pharmacy director's job very, very difficult. Rick's challenge in his chosen field, pharmacy administration, was that the director's job was one of only two or three like it in the entire city. Waiting for another opportunity didn't seem too promising unless he was willing to totally relocate, and he refused that option. We discussed consulting. Within two weeks, he had set up a complete home office. So badly did he want to move on that he approached several organizations about consulting. He pitched a small, growing pharmaceutical company that had a new product it would introduce in six months. Rick didn't want to wait that long. He pitched the idea of becoming a consultant for them immediately. He stressed the benefits and value. They were persuaded. He got a part-time contract for about 15 to 20 hours per week, with a guarantee of $4,000 per month. He also picked up another small project. Both projects together would total about 20 hours per week, but still less salary than his current job. To quit was a significant risk. His income would drop unless he obtained more work. And he'd have no benefits, which would add to his need for additional salary. Rumors spread throughout the hospital that a massive layoff was imminent. We talked about the possibility of getting a severance package for Rick. He hesitated. I clearly remember saying: "If you are waiting for a guarantee, it'll never come. Whenever you go off on your own, there will always be *risk.* The severance package eases the way—but there is still a significant risk." Rick said he did want a "guarantee" because he was a cautious man when it came to his family's financial security. I also warned him that the severance package would not always be available to shoulder the path. Rick decided to leave. He approached the personnel department to discuss the options. He'd prepared his persuasion package and discussed it with human resources: The need for more layoffs in his department could be reduced if he left. Being an administrator, his departure would save two other jobs, as his salary was significantly higher than those of the staff pharmacists. He'd created a package and a persuasion campaign that made it easy for the hospital management to let him go. He was officially laid off, but as part of his severance package, he'd successfully negotiated six months' salary and 18 months of paid benefits. In *one day,* he changed the entire direction of his life and career. Losing the coveted job made him realize that if he wanted to move ahead, he'd have to go elsewhere.

Rick was industrious. Within four months, the smaller company he'd been consulting with offered him a full-time vice president's job. He used the salary negotiation techniques you'll learn in this book to really advance his situation: His new base salary of $80,000 was $15,000 more than that of the hospital job he'd left. Bonuses would be tied to the company's and the department's success. During his first year, his bonus was an additional $13,000. The change proved to be terrific for him. Rick loved the fast-paced environment as his new company rolled out a new product he was directly in charge of. Choices—Rick made some good ones. His willingness to take a risk turned out to be the best move of his entire career.

## *Promotions*

Opportunities can come in two packages: *internal* (inside your current organization) or *external* (from a new company).

You must size up the possibilities inside your company and department. Identify all the key areas and the potential jobs you'd like to hold. Recruit some allies and even a mentor or adviser. Not all situations resolve into a promotion like my client Whitney's did. Rick's promotional career track got stymied when someone else took over the director's chair. He elected to go elsewhere. Only you can decide when you've had enough and want to find a new employer offering better career opportunities for you. But look carefully before you leap. In very large companies, ask several managers and bosses their ideas and advice on what you need to do to move ahead. Then you can decide whether it is worth it to move full-speed ahead or better to move to a new organization.

## All Is Not Fair in Corporate Promotions

You may find that there is a time when you simply do not get the next job because of a hidden political agenda. Your company may want to promote a minority or a woman—and that's not you. There are times when the most-qualified person does not get the job, times when someone less qualified or even (in your mind) incompetent gets promoted. We've all seen it happen. If it's happened to you, then you need to take a long hard look at your goals and your organization. Now may be the time to make your decisions. Discreetly get a better feel for what other managers and department heads think about the company, you, and a new position. Inquire about what you might need to do to improve your chances for the next promotion. You may find your boss is *not* your biggest supporter. He or she may want you to remain exactly where you are right now: working on that individual's team. The boss's help may be nonexistent in that case. Another possibility is that your manager simply may not like you that much. There are times when your boss may not be in a good position to help you even if he or she wanted to. Your boss may have dropped out of favor with upper management. Some bosses may be coasting in their jobs, allowing your area to be seen as an insignificant innovator or producer. Personal problems (e.g., divorce or an ill family member) can preoccupy their lives, leaving few reserves to help you. Some bosses have relatively little power in the overall structure of the organization. The bottom line for you is that you must play the cards you are dealt. Seek advice, gather information, and sort out your options, alternatives, and the potential consequences of your choices and actions. Then decide on your plan of action.

PROMOTION POSSIBILITIES ASSESSMENT

1. Size up the company, its parent, and subsidiaries for opportunities.

2. Identify new growth areas, new product development or expansion, or management changes. These offer the best options for promotional opportunities.

3. Evaluate the role your boss and your boss's boss can or will play in your career advancement.

4. Develop an internal network outside your department to increase your insider information on job options.

5. Develop your strategies and action plans.

6. Implement strategies.

7. Evaluate results.

8. Reevaluate options if no promotion develops within six months.

## New Job

For many of my clients the fastest way to move their careers ahead was to obtain a new job. The big salary increases are often obtained by jumping to a new employer. You may try using a dual approach: Look at both internal opportunities and other companies.

The key elements to finding a better job are savvy job-hunting skills, a strong resumé, and a good persuasion package. When looking for a new position, be selective about the opportunity. Thoroughly explore the company before you accept any offer. Be sure it will be a good match for you and your goals. Today, with many jobs residing with small employers, you may have a good job, or even a terrific job, but the company is so small that the only opportunity to move up is to move *on*.

The most important first step in looking for a new job is to have a clear idea of the job target you want. You can't fully focus your efforts until you are clear which job title (e.g., systems analyst, trainer, marketing coordinator) you are going after. You must decipher all your skills that relate to doing the desired job and then select the most promising to promote in your resumé, cover letter, and in the interview. The charts and assessments in the previous pages of this chapter are designed to help you develop a clear idea of exactly what you are looking for.

# *Entrepreneurialism*

Helping people was something Gail Lohr always wanted to do. She spent 13 years as a hospital social worker. She liked her job, the security, the hours, and the benefits. Gail's career was settled, but she and her husband faced a common problem—they could never save any money. With three daughters they wanted to someday send to college, they thought of a very creative solution. The Lohrs would buy a home and rent it out. The rent would cover the mortgage, expenses, and taxes. The house itself would act as a "college bank account" that would accumulate dollars as they paid off the mortgage. They bought one house, then another, and decided that in order to obtain the best deals on new home listings, it would be best if Gail got her real estate license. She did this. Much to Gail's surprise, other people quickly learned that she was a real estate agent, and she became an instantaneous success in her new field.

Her business grew so fast that she had to decide whether to remain at her secure job or go for broke as a real estate agent whose only salary came from sales commissions. As she contemplated her decision, one fact surprised her—she really enjoyed helping people who wanted her assistance. A challenge her hospital social worker job continuously handed her was the resistance from patients and families who didn't want to be sick or face hard, painful decisions. The draw of helping others who really wanted help was seductive. She quit and went into real estate full-time. Within one year, she was the #1 sales producer. While Gail loved her new job, her husband Gary hated his. An accountant with 70-hour workweeks, high pressure, and stress, he constantly complained. When his company sought to restructure, Gail encouraged him to accept the early retirement option. So, at age 43, Gary Lohr retired. He spent a few months considering his career path, and then opportunity knocked: The owners of Gail's Century 21 office offered to sell their business to the Lohrs. Gail was reluctant; she worried about the financial risk; ownership scared her. But Gary was so happy about the idea of being a business manager that they went ahead. That decision changed their lives. Three years later, they've tripled their net worth and built the company into the biggest one in their region, even as the local economy plummeted.

The possibility of self-employment needs to be explored as a potential career option. You can move along in your career as Gail did, then have opportunity just knock as it did for her. She did indeed buy the company she'd been working for and has seen tremendous financial rewards and personal success as a result.

If you do not choose to be a traditional employee, consider the following options:

1. Start own your business.

2. Buy an ongoing business or franchise.

3. Open a home-based business.

4. Be a consultant.

5. Try contract work.

## Start Your Own Business

One way to guarantee your job security is to become your own boss and open a business. According to the Small Business Administration, 819,477 Americans started their own businesses during the last year.

Running a business needs strong determination to maintain your drive through the thousands of hours you'll need to get your business turned into a profitable enterprise.

### BUSINESS OWNERSHIP ASSESSMENT

1. *Are you a self-starter?* It will be up to you, not someone else, to develop the business, organize the projects, manage your time, follow through on details.

2. *Can you handle the uncertain financial risk?* Businesses all have cycles, ebbs, and flows in their profitability. Once it's started, you'll have overhead and operational expenses that must be met before you get paid.

3. *Do you have good business skills in the areas of business planning, sales, marketing, and customer service?* You must get customers. The need for new and repeat customers is your business's lifeblood. You must possess or learn these skills to survive and succeed.

4. *Do you have the stamina to run a business?* Business ownership is a lot of work. Can you face 12-hour workdays, six or seven days a week, every week?

5. *Are you motivated by achievement?* Many entrepreneurs get a great joy out of the daily "wins" they get in doing business. They find it's a competitive game and a satisfying way to fulfill their instinct to achieve, and they have fun doing it. These people have

a passion and driving desire to come in first. They are doers. They want to see evidence derived from their efforts and labor. They are unlikely to get burned out or worn down by carrying all the responsibilities of the business on their shoulders.

6. *Are you a good decision maker?*   Business owners are required to make decisions constantly, quickly, under pressure, and independently. Do you research and examine all options on important decisions to minimize your risk, but then decide to go forward?

7. *How well do you handle different personalities?*   Business owners need to develop working relationships with a variety of people, including customers, vendors, staff, bankers, and professionals such as lawyers, accountants, or graphic artists. Your degree of success in dealing with a demanding client, an unreliable vendor, or a cranky staff person will directly impact your business.

8. *How will the business affect your family?*   The first few years of business start-up can be hard to balance against the demands of family life. There may also be financial difficulties until the business becomes profitable, which could take months or years. You may have to adjust to a lower standard of living or put family assets at risk. Can your family deal with the challenges business ownership requires? Although many entrepreneurs go on to make large incomes, the lean years are a necessary part of the evolution and business growth cycle.

## THE POSITIVES OF BUSINESS OWNERSHIP

✔ You are the boss.

✔ Hard work and long hours can benefit you personally rather than increasing profits for someone else.

✔ Your income potential and growth are far less limited.

✔ Running a business allows for creating excitement, variety, and challenge.

✔ You control your own destiny.

Consider this quick overview of the steps you'll need to take to get your own business idea off the ground:

✔ *Select carefully.*   There are a mountain of options to choose from when you consider what kind of business to open. *Do your research.* Look at the business's potential; evaluate the types of customers as well as the start-up and operational costs. Examine your potential competitors. Visit their organizations, review their marketing and sales material, and get a list of their prices or fees. Interview and learn from people who already operate the type of business you want to pursue. William Stolze's *Start Up* (Career Press) is a great book that covers all the fundamentals. Also call for a free resource guide available from the Small Business Administration. Look in the government listings to locate an office near you. You'll need to develop a business plan, budgets, and possibly take out a loan to get your business started. Counselors at the Small Business Administration can be quite helpful in these preliminary stages.

✔ *Have realistic expectations.*   During the first five years 80% of all new businesses fail or close. This can be attributed to two major reasons: (1) The business was underfinanced. (2) The owner underestimated the long hours required to operate the business, and the take-home profit was much lower than hoped for.

All businesses have overhead (telephones, office equipment, taxes, advertising expenses) that must be paid before the owner. A solid business plan that includes conservative growth and realistic budgets is a much needed road map to your success.

✔ *Conserve resources as you set up the office operations.*   Many new businesses need capital during the first three or four years before they ever break a profit. It's advisable to have at least six months of additional funding past your designated breakeven date.

Get professional help to set up your accounting records. You must be thorough in your understanding of taxes and license requirements that you will now be required to pay. *Quick Books,* by Intuit, is a good software program for new small businesses.

Buy used equipment and replace it as your income grows. You can often do without a copier or a fancy phone—but spend your dollars where they are warranted. Your business may need a state-of-the-art computer system to allow you to create marketing pieces, correspondence, and invoices and to track sales.

Identify vendors that are reasonable and nearby. For example, using a copy machine at your local Mailboxes store and a discount printer for letterhead, cards, and flyers can add up to significant savings.

✔ *Research your market.*   You'll spend 90% of your time looking for and trying to attract customers. Collect ideas from colleagues, friends, and other businesses that might be adapted to work for you. Read books on sales, marketing, direct mail, and advertising. Above all else, test for results before you invest large sums of money in any marketing endeavor. A lot will change during your first year of operation. Consider printing smaller quantities or using the predesigned papers available at local paper stores as you develop your niche and market focus.

## Home-Based Business

There are 25 million Americans who operate businesses from their homes. The advantages include the following:

✔ Lower overhead

✔ No lost commuting time

✔ Convenience

✔ More personal profits

✔ Lower or more modest start-up costs

The negative stereotype of "working from home" has disappeared as savvy entrepreneurs see this to be a good option—in many cases, the only option available.

The single biggest complication is how your business will impact your family and personal life. Motivated, driven people never worry about being distracted with house stuff to avoid business responsibilities. On the contrary, they often find that the ease of going to the "office" equates to working *all the time.* Your business will never be out of sight. Even if a closed-off room is passed by—you'll know work is waiting. You must set parameters that you and your family can live with. A separate phone line, designated hours, and respect for your work time are essential. For more information on operating a business from home, read Paul and Sarah Edwards' books, *Working from Home, The Best Home Business for the 90s,* and *Getting Business to Come to You.*

## Consulting

You must have an area of expertise in which you specialize. Most consultants have had extensive experience in their field. They serve many clients or just a few. As downsizing rocked America throughout the '90s, many 40- and 50-year-olds found themselves "consulting" because few other options were available.

The best sources of business are former employers and referrals from current satisfied clients. Repeat business is the mainstay for many consultants. Consulting may be less demanding than businesses that sell products, but savvy marketing skills to land assignments will always be essential. Professional services are the most common: financial, strategic planning, human resources, marketing, public relations, training, project management, or industry-specific expertise.

## Contract Worker

This is not business ownership. Instead, you are employed by a temporary agency to work in another company. It's common for engineers, systems analysts, computer programmers, and trainers to be contract workers. Salaries are comparable to those of in-house employees, but often include no benefits or simply medical/dental options that the temporary company offers. As more of the country's larger employers respond to business cycles and global competition, expect the numbers of professional contract workers to grow. This position is a terrific deal for the company, but can leave you with limited promotion options and no retirement benefits. It may be better as a temporary solution, not a long-term career commitment, depending on your individual circumstances and needs.

## *Your Future Possibilities*

We've explored the options, available—promotion, new job, entrepreneurialism (own or home-based business, consulting, or contractor worker). Now define your goals.

**DEFINE SHORT-TERM CAREER GOAL**

_____

_____

_____

_____

_____

_____

_____

## SET LONG-TERM CAREER GOAL

_____

_____

_____

_____

_____

_____

_____

## SKILLS NEEDED TO ACQUIRE

**How:** _____

_____

**Where:** _____

_____

**Time frame:** _____

_____

**My goal for you: a position that makes you happy and brings you a great deal of satisfaction.**

Now that you've completed this chapter, you have your essential skills and long-term game plan in mind. If you want to make it into the echelons of top management, good career planning and decision making are essential. Business ownership requires the same. Best of all, you can always reevaluate your options and change your mind.

## DESIRE

*You can have anything you want if you want it desperately enough. By sheer determination and will, your actions will guide you beyond your dreams to achieve more than you ever thought possible.*

*Dream big. Life is made up of wanting something, taking risks, failing sometimes, but winning more often than not. No one can stop you but you.*

*Achieve—not to impress others—but for yourself. Because in the achievements are the inner joys and satisfactions that make living and working worthwhile.*

—ROBIN RYAN

Ever wonder why another job hunter landed the job you interviewed for and you didn't? Or why a coworker was selected for a job and you were passed over? Why does another employee succeed in getting a raise and you don't? Why can your friend seem to be able to negotiate for a higher salary and perks and you can't?

The answers to these questions could bolster your career: The key is your ability to persuade. Your presentation of yourself, your skills, and requests to employers must be memorable, positive, and put forth with perfect timing, using proven tools. Three primary factors influence how others perceive you: *substance, timing,* and *style.* All three are essential for your success.

*Substance* emphasizes the quantitative proof of your value and accomplishments. Whether you're in an interview, a salary negotiation, a performance review, or asking for a raise, the following tools should be part of your career arsenal:

Each of these tools will help you pinpoint the employer's position in relationship to your career opportunities. (More on these tools will follow shortly.)

| CAREER TOOLBOX |
| --- |
| *60 Second Sell* |
| *5 Point Agenda* |
| *Informational Interview* |
| *Hiring Chart* |
| *Salary Extractor* |
| *Productivity Monitor* |
| *Performance Chart* |

*Timing* is an important element in influencing how people perceive you. *When* you ask for a raise is equally as important as *how* you ask for a raise. There are deadly times to avoid. We'll offer advice to pick the time that's paramount to your success.

*Style* is both the look and attire you select and present. It's the foundation of your communication and delivery. Style is an important factor savvy job hunters incorporate to confidently project themselves. Choose your interview outfit to radiate a "look of success." Additionally, successful people recognize that using the correct tone, words, emphasis, energy, and enthusiasm literally "make the man or woman."

The key to successful persuasion is selecting the appropriate tools, phrases, and delivery style that will be well received by the employer or boss. Persuasion can take two roads: positive or negative. According to psychologist Dr. Herbert Clark, the average person will understand a positive statement twice as fast as a negative statement. Your communications will be more effective if you consistently center them around positive, logical, concrete formats. Additionally, you must incorporate the use of "we" into your arguments, conversations, or statements. Today's workplace demands individual accountability for the team to reach company goals. "Self-directed team" is a common buzzword. Managers and upper management are judged on how they get the project done. They are evaluated on their efforts to motivate and direct the group to get good results. Keeping the "we" concept in mind, you must also operate from a win-win position. By addressing the employer's needs ("here's what you get if I join the team"), you'll be better able to show why the proposed idea (new job, promotion, or salary) is a good idea for both parties.

## The Tools

**All of the persuasion tools are market-tested with proven successful results.**

My persuasion strategies and techniques are essential tools to manage your career, whether you are looking for a job as vice president or seeking your very first position. You will need to develop and use these tools during job interviews, salary and raise negotiations, and to influence promotions.

The tools you are about to learn have a long track record of success. They have been used by numerous clients and seminar participants, who have reported that these tools helped them land the job or the raise they wanted. They are easily learned and applied. These will become important tools in your career management arsenal.

On the next few pages I'll define each tool and explain when and how they are used. In later chapters, you'll sit in on interviews and salary discussions to learn firsthand how my clients have used these tools to get hired, promoted, and obtain more money or perks.

## CAREER TOOLBOX—
## 60 Second Sell™

Of all the techniques and strategies I've taught, it's the 60 Second Sell that I get the most feedback on, stating that it was the most valuable and useful tool in people's successful job search. This technique really hones your most important skills and accomplishments into just a few phrases that will meet the employer's needs. The 60 Second Sell is used to open and close the interview as well as answer certain tough questions the interviewer might throw at you.

**The 60 Second Sell is your verbal business card.**

### THE TECHNIQUE

Analyze the job and the duties needed to perform the job well. Correlate those to the employer's needs, and select your top five selling points to meet the needs. Link these five points together in a few sentences: This is your 60 Second Sell.

### PURPOSE

The 60 Second Sell is a *memorized and customized statement* to direct the employer's attention to your top skills. It will quickly engage the employer and tell him or her that you are a viable and top candidate for the job. Too often, job hunters assume the employer is listening to every word they say with bated breath. Not true! In fact, at my seminars I ask every manager who has hired someone to raise a hand. Typically, 100 hands go up. I then say, "If you agree with this statement keep your hand up: 'You can interview someone for 20 minutes and not hear a word they say.' " No hands go down. That's revealing, since your first objective in the interview is to get the employer to listen to you. By immediately focusing the interviewer on your top skills and accomplishments, you get the employer's full attention.

**USES**

1. Use the 60 Second Sell in the opening minute if at all possible. It is the perfect response when the employer says, *"Tell me about yourself."*

2. Close the interview by reminding the employer of your most marketable strengths. Use it at the very end after you've learned what the rest of the process will be and asked all your questions of the employer. Start with the words, "Thank you for this opportunity to meet with you today. I'm most interested in your position. Before I go let me summarize for you what I'd bring to this position . . . now insert your 60 Second Sell.

3. Use the 60 Second Sell to answer the following kinds of questions: *"What are your strengths?" "What are your proudest accomplishments?" "Why should I hire you?"*

**EXAMPLE**

Ed was a telecommunications program manager who excelled at building partnerships and accomplishing more than expected with his budgets, staff, and resources. Here is the 60 Second Sell he used to land a new job at a more prestigious organization:

> I've spent the last 12 years developing new partnerships and product service programs for my company. As a result of the team's efforts, we have increased capacity and usage by 30%. I attribute this success to a couple of factors. The first is my ability to create self-directed teams, where goals are clear and job accountability enables each person to maximize their productivity. Next we jointly tackle problems to find customer-oriented solutions. This approach has reduced customer complaints by 50% and retains a higher number of current clients from moving to competitors. I pride myself on some pretty savvy negotiations skills. Even though my multimillion-dollar budget has been decreased by 12%, we've acquired concessions and better terms from vendors, plus some reorganizing for more efficient systems to accomplish more with less funds. In a nutshell, this is the experience I'd bring to the job.

**ADAPTATIONS**

Savvy job hunters realize that you may glean insightful information during the interview. Ed, our telecommunications manager whose 60 Second Sell you just read, was continually asked during his interview about computer systems and processes he'd used. Noting that this was important to the employer, Ed changed his 60 Second Sell as he closed the interview. He did this by replacing one point and substituting a new point, noting his strengths in computer systems. The five points used in the 60 Second Sell make up the 5 Point Agenda.

## CAREER TOOLBOX—
## 5 Point Agenda™

This hiring strategy allows you to prepare in a fast but highly effective manner. This technique can also be easily adapted during the interview if you've gathered new insight into the employer's specific needs. This technique identifies your top five selling points to perform and excel at the employer's job.

**The 5 Point Agenda markets your five top selling points.**

### THE TECHNIQUE

Analyze the employer's job and determine your five most marketable strengths to perform the job. Repeatedly weave these points throughout the interviews in answers with concrete, specific examples.

### PURPOSE

Most employers can remember only a few specifics about each interviewed applicant. The 5 Point Agenda is a way to ensure that the employer will clearly remember five specific points about you once you depart from the interview. By selecting your five top selling points and weaving them into your answers throughout the interview, the employer will note and remember important information about you.

What are the five points that you want the employer to remember about you? Analyze what's important in the job and what you bring to the job. It might be your experience, your strengths in certain areas, your background with numbers, your organizational abilities, or your supervisory skills. It could be anything, as long as it is a key component to performing the employer's job. To determine what would be most important to the employer, analyze the duties you think are needed to perform the job. Then consider any inside information about the employer's major concerns that you've uncovered during your research or from your contacts. Write out the specific duties you know are necessary to do the job. Then make a list of your five major points. Study these and weave them into your answers. Repetition is all right because it will help the employer remember key information. Your five points are your self-marketing strategy. They'll help you focus on presenting your best abilities to the employer.

## USES

1. Customized for each interview by predetermining the employer's needs.
2. You direct the interview and focus on demonstrated accomplishments when answering questions.

## EXAMPLE

Here is Ed's 5 Point Agenda for a position as a telecommunications program manager:

1. Twelve years' program management experience
2. Increased capacity and usage by 30%
3. Developed productive self-directed teams
4. Customer service–orientated with track recording for improving satisfaction
5. Savvy negotiations and budget management skills

When Ed adapted these points toward his close, he stressed the computer systems. He felt he could drop the emphasis on building teams, since he'd already made that point and the interviewer seemed much more interested in the computer systems background.

**Informational interviews uncover unadvertised job openings.**

## CAREER TOOLBOX—
## Informational Interview

85% of all jobs are *never* advertised . . . 85%! Most of those are the good jobs with the better salaries that you seek. Informational interviewing is a proven technique that job hunters have used for years. Although it's been popular since the mid-'80s, I still find that 40 to 50% of people in my job search classes are unfamiliar with it.

## THE TECHNIQUE

Arrange and conduct a short, 15 to 20 minute interview to learn more about potential job openings, valued skills, and companies.

## PURPOSE

There are several levels of effective informational interviewing. The basic level seeks insight and researches a career field, a new industry, or a career change. In this kind of interviewing, you want to talk to people who are actually doing the job that you'd like to do in the field that you'd like to be in. You try to assess what the job duties are and the skills needed for the position.

You explore salary, educational requirements, and the normal career track to get this kind of position. You seek to learn how someone might enter the field or advance an existing career in the industry. *Basic informational interviewing* allows you to gather some knowledge to determine whether you want to change fields, enter a new field, or work in a specific industry.

*Secondary informational interviewing* is uncovering organizational structure, locations, departments, products, and decision makers' names, as well as discovering where job openings might be. Ask questions that give you names of new contacts who are employed in the job you want or who work for a prospective company you are interested in. Any contact at a company can give you insight into the company culture: how they do their hiring, where your job might fall in the organizational structure, who might hire for that kind of position. Additionally, you want to get the names of the hiring decision makers.

*Primary informational interviewing* is setting up appointments with the people who have the power to hire you in the organizations where you wish to work. This is where you are learning the needs of your potential boss and the skills he or she values. This is the stage that many of you may jump to immediately. Your conversations will uncover job leads and important selling points employers care about.

## USES

To obtain needed information on unadvertised jobs and skills desired, the most effective steps are as follows:

✔ Establish initial appointments through referral from another person via introductory letter or phone call.

✔ Opening comments or purpose for contact can be varied.
—Would like advice on job search.
—Discuss vocational interest.
—Desire information on field, industry, or geographical area.

✔ Reassure the person that you don't expect him or her to have a job opening or even know about a job—that you are simply looking for guidance and input to help you better direct your job search.

✔ Be specific about time being requested (usually 15 minutes).

✔ Prepare for the interview. Read company and agency literature. Know what information you plan to request. Write out your questions.
—Duties of person, major responsibilities, salary ranges.
—Functions or structure of organization.
—Trends in field.
—Procedures, products, programs used or being developed.
—Sources for additional information.
—Suggestions for entry or development into a particular position, field, industry, or company.

✔ Make a positive impression.
—Arrive early for your interview.
—Dress well.
—Introduce yourself to receptionist.
—Consider having a business card.
—Have a resumé and references available in case you are asked.

At the start of the meeting, reintroduce yourself and your reason for being there. Summarize your background and credentials in the first 60 seconds. This will save time and allow you to ask specific questions and get answers in the time allotted. Be sure to ask for referrals to others you could contact. Get suggestions on other companies to approach. Some contacts will be more helpful than others. If you go past the agreed-upon time, offer to arrange a second meeting (by phone) so as not to inconvenience the contact or cause that person to work overtime because you took too much time. And always send a handwritten thank-you note immediately after the interview meeting.

**EXAMPLE**

Cathy seeks a new position in the corporate communications area. She obtained Tom Johnson's name from a friend. She wrote Tom a brief letter of introduction to request an informational interview. She follows up by calling Tom to arrange the meeting. This was her approach:

"Good afternoon, Bank America Corporate Communications."
"Tom Johnson, please. This is Cathy Saunders calling."
"May I tell him what this is in regard to?"

"Of course, I'm following up to arrange a meeting."

"One moment, please . . ."

"Tom Johnson."

"Hello Tom, this is Cathy Saunders. Jim McDonald suggested I contact you to arrange a brief meeting—I sent you a letter last week—by chance have you read it yet?"

"I do remember seeing something."

"Great. Jim had suggested that I meet with you to get your advice on my current job search. I've spent the last eight years as First Interstate Bank's communication specialist, and with the recent merger and all, I'm now job hunting. Jim felt you'd be a terrific contact to advise me, but let me reassure you, Tom, I don't expect you to have a job or even know about a job. It's only advice I seek. Could you spare 15 minutes next Tuesday or is Wednesday better?"

"Well, Wednesday's easier."

"Morning or afternoon?"

"Let's say 4:30 P.M."

"Great—I can easily stop by then. Could you transfer me to the receptionist for directions?"

"Wouldn't it be easier to do this by phone?"

"Well, I thought that I could show you a bit of my work. I produced the company's newsletter and annual report. You might find it insightful to see what we did."

"Okay—4:30 P.M. here—I'll connect you to Liz and she'll give you directions and explain about parking."

"Thanks, Tom. I'll see you next Wednesday at 4:30 P.M."

## IDEAL VERSUS PRACTICAL

In a perfect world you would find every contact opening up his or her door and letting you drop by. They'd offer wonderful insights and several job leads, plus extend contacts names. Many of my clients find this is exactly what happens. But sometimes busy executives are reluctant to invite you to their office. In the past, people may have overstayed their welcome, resulting in one or even two hours of lost time for the executive. Therefore, contacts may be cautious or need to monitor their time more wisely due to their own job demands. Be open to both face-to-face meetings or simple telephone chats. You can learn a lot either way. The better option is to be able to "see" inside the

**CAREER COACH** *fact*

*The Department of Labor states that two-thirds of all jobs found in the last year were uncovered through contacts.*

employer, but you may not be able to get away to do that too often if you are still working elsewhere.

Informative interviewing is a type of networking that is a very effective way to learn about both openings and the exact skills employers value and hire for.

## *Increase Your Competitive Advantage*

Contacts developed through the informational interview phase can be very helpful when a real interview comes along. You can call back anyone who might have some "insider information" to pass onto you. Their insights can be an important shaper in developing your emphasis in your 5 Point Agenda and 60 Second Sell. This is how many candidates are able to land the job even when others have better qualifications on their resumés. They use this insider info to convince the employer they know exactly what needs to be done and how they can do it. Of course, you must be honest in your claims. Integrity is a highly prized personal trait all employers look for.

### CAREER TOOLBOX—
### Hiring Chart™

This is a new and sophisticated tool. It allows you to dissect the company's needs for a particular job and at the same time illustrate how you can meet those needs. It's an easy reference by which an employer can measure skills and job performance.

**The Hiring Chart illustrates the needed skills that the employer wants.**

### THE TECHNIQUE
Create a two-column T-shaped chart that lists the job needs on the left and your skills, abilities, and past experience performing the corresponding duties on the right.

### PURPOSE
The Hiring Chart is used to clarify the most important skills the employer wants for a particular job.

### USES
1. When conducting your informational interviews, you might take your preliminary Hiring Chart to show potential employers. Tell

them, "I believe these are the needs this company has if it is going to hire someone for this kind of position. Is it accurate? Have I hit on anything that isn't really important to you? Is there anything I've overlooked that you would consider important?"

Remember, you're talking to either the person who has the power to hire you or to the one who has the kind of job you want. This person's insight can offer a crucial piece of information. Perhaps you missed an important skill or ability that you didn't realize the employer would value on that job. Perhaps supervising others might be important, or detailing computer skills would be vital. You need to know what the employer considers important. Adjust your chart based on the things the employer tells you. Later, analyze the experience that you have to offer in that particular area. Illustrate your experiences in the contributions area. Your Hiring Chart can be used every time you're talking to a hiring employer. You'll want to verify with several employers that they all see the listed skills as important. You may learn of an important skill each hiring manager mentions that you do not have. Use this information to reevaluate the job you want to target. Assess your options on how to obtain any lacking skill. Often, a seminar or books can round out the profile employers prefer. If indeed they require an MBA and you lack one, recognize that you might have to refocus your goals. Be sure all hiring managers are requiring MBAs. Often, job hunters think one thing ("I don't need an MBA"), but hiring managers think a different way ("This position needs an MBA"). During the informational interview, use your Hiring Chart as a learning process to focus your skills and experiences on what the hiring employer wants.

2. You'll develop a fairly sophisticated tool; then your approach to employers can vary: "These are the needs as I assessed them. Here are the contributions I can make. Can you think of any companies or organizations that have a specific need for someone with this background?" You will find your Hiring Chart generates many job leads.

3. The Hiring Chart is a strong self-marketing tool that you can take to an interview. At the start of the interview, take out your Hiring Chart and say, "I've broken down the components I feel are needed for this job." *Customize the chart to each company's specific needs.* Then go over your contributions and get the

employer's feedback. You'll impress the employer and he or she will remember you.

4. A Hiring Chart can be an influential tool during the salary negotiation phase. As you discuss the job, you can pull out your Hiring Chart to go over the needed duties and use the contribution section to quantify to the employer *why* you are worth more money. This "proof" can be an important aid in securing a higher starting salary or more benefits, such as an additional week of vacation or a relocation package or signing bonus.

**EXAMPLE**

Nancy earned $32,000 as a graphic designer. She wanted another position in a progressive company's design department. This Hiring Chart was a powerful tool she left behind after the both informational and actual interviews. Indeed, she got the coveted job of her dreams, beating out hundreds of other graphic designers to land the job, with a $4,000 salary increase.

**GRAPHIC DESIGNER—NANCY ELLERSTON**

| Needs | Contributions |
|---|---|
| Computer Skills | Proficiency on Macintosh and PC systems utilizing PageMaker, Photoshop, Adobe Illustrator, Freehand, Pagemill, Word. |
| Flier, Brochure, and Ad Designs | Created over 500 trade ads, brochures, and fliers to market products and services. |
| Newsletter | Designed monthly 4-page, 2-color newsletter. Coordinated with writer and marketing staff. Increased product sales with repeat customers by 10%. |
| Web Design | Designed graphics and all page layouts on company's web site. |
| Print Coordination | Produced mechanicals and Linotronic outputs for printer. Provided color ink/paper advisement. Performed blue line and press checks on printing projects. |
| Communication Skills | Worked with hundreds of clients both internal and external to ascertain needs and produce acceptable finished products. |
| Time Management | Simultaneously handled multiple projects, always coming in on deadline and within or under budget. |

## CAREER TOOLBOX—
# Salary Extractor™

We would all like to make more money. The key to achieving this goal is to determine the maximum amount that the employer can and will pay for the job you are doing. A secret to success in all salary negotiations: Let the employer be the first one to throw out a salary figure. In Chapter 8, we'll go into detail about the whole salary negotiation process. But for now, remember never to list any previous salary on an application. Never bring up or offer the salary amount you desire in a cover letter or during the interview. *Whoever mentions money first loses.* Don't let it be you if you are determined to get a salary increase.

*CAREER COACH tip*

**The Salary Extractor obtains the highest dollar amount the employer will pay you.**

### THE TECHNIQUE

Never mention any salary figure before the employer does. Always get the employer to pinpoint exactly how much they will pay you by volleying back questions and having salary surveys to substantiate your desired salary.

### PURPOSE

Using this technique will help you obtain the highest possible salary and desired benefits package.

### USES

During the interview, when the employer inquires what salary you seek, deflect the question. First try to volley back with your own question: "Exactly what is the range that this job pays?" If you are pressed for a figure, reply with a survey figure, for example, "According to the National Association of Management Accountants, for an accounting manager with nine years of manufacturing experience the salary would range between $42,000 and $70,000. That's the range I'd expect this job would pay." Then move on.

Establish your value *first;* then negotiate salary *after* you've been offered the job.

### EXAMPLES

Chapter 8 has detailed examples and case studies of clients using the Salary Extractor to negotiate better compensation packages.

## CAREER TOOLBOX—
# Productivity Monitor™

It's very important to document skills and accomplishments on the job. These become essential when asking for a raise or when competing for a promotion. These activity records are the basic make-up of future resumés—so keep the skills and accomplishments detailed with size, numbers, percentages, increases, or decreases. Note any cost or time savings.

### THE TECHNIQUE

Generate a monthly record of work accomplishments and activities that substantiate your on-the-job contributions.

**Your record of on-the-job productivity influences raises and promotions.**

### PURPOSE

Using the Productivity Monitor will enable you to track your career accomplishments.

### USES

1. For performance reviews, you can duplicate your list and give it to your boss for your review. It can be quite effective to remind bosses of forgotten contributions.

2. This document shows the "proof" or "evidence" of your performance and productivity to justify a raise or salary increase.

3. This can be used to show job growth and adaptability to handle new duties as you seek an internal promotion.

4. This tool documents accomplishments when they are recently completed to note important contributions to be added to your resumé. Statistics, numbers, percentages, and savings should all be noted.

### EXAMPLES

Jane was a regional sales manager. One-third of her bonus was tied to "outreach and new marketing activities." Her Productivity Monitor was an important record of the numerous things she brought to her company. Over the years, her Productivity Monitor has helped her get a raise even in years when most other senior managers didn't.

## PRODUCTIVITY MONITOR

| Month | Activity |
|---|---|
| January | Hired new rep for California. Trained rep on new selling techniques and introduced to client. Rep made first month's quotas. Planned/organized marketing strategies for spring trade show. |
| February | Major blitz promoting trade show. Did weekly postcard mailers. Held rep retreat, offered motivational speaker, set new goals. Tackled rep problems, attitude killers. |
| March | Coordinated all activities for trade show. Produced 17 strong leads for new RL equipment. Got some testimonials on product to use in direct mail campaign. |
| April | Sold 3 RLs off trade show list. Reps working on two others. Did presentation for top management. Organized training sessions on RL for client's staff. |
| May | Hired two new reps. Changed bonus structure and began personal motivation strategy, sending incentives via e-mail. Reps liked it. |
| June | Trained new reps and assisted with 2 RL salespeople in their territories. Total of 5 so far. Will exceed the goal of eight for year. Did postcard blitz on summer conference. |
| July | Arranged all the details with hotel for one week, learning new computer system at client's conference. Included 10 new, fun activities to increase attendance from 45. goal is 70. |
| August | Sent color brochure on conference and fun activities. Had reps personally call every client to invite them. Sold 1 RL. Organized e-mail and videoconferencing rep meetings. |
| September | Conference got 91 attendees. Clients loved Vegas shows and activities. Sold 3 RLs during conference. Hit year-end goal. Set up major bonus if two more are sold. |
| October | Sold 1 RL. Set up sales incentive and major bonus to rep who sells any RL for before year-end. Reorganized paperwork process for online e-mail transmission. |
| November | Got it—sold 1 RL to group who came for Vegas trip. Added another day of staff training to better meet clients' needs. Did year-end reports. |
| December | Planned Christmas party. Added luncheon and Santa. Mailed direct mail flyers on Christmas stock—leftover bolstered end-of-month sales by 12%. Planned new sales goals with VP. Gave to reps. |

Total RLs sold: 11

## MAJOR RESUMÉ ACCOMPLISHMENTS FOR THE YEAR

- Sold 11 RLs (quota 8) achieved 140% over quota.
- Moved region to #2 in sales revenues from #8 (14 total regions).
- Received corporate outstanding-manager-of-year award.
- Implemented computer system for online sales reports.
- Saved reps 5 hours per week; reduced costs by 22%.

## IMPLEMENTATION

This is an important tool to record your activities. You can simply high-light the major points, as Jane did, or you can be more detailed on daily/weekly activities. Create your tracking device to aid you in substantiating and "reminding" your organization just how valuable and indispensable you are.

## PRODUCTIVITY MONITOR

**January**

_____

_____

**February**

_____

_____

**March**

_____

_____

**April**

_____

_____

**May**

_____

_____

**June**

_____

_____

**July**

**August**

**September**

**October**

**November**

**December**

## RESUMÉ ENHANCER

A major advantage of the Productivity Monitor is that you actually write down significant contributions to be noted on your resumé. Update your resumé every six months. For more help on resumés, consult my book, *Winning Resumés,* published by John Wiley & Sons.

## MAJOR RESUMÉ ACCOMPLISHMENTS FOR THE YEAR

- 
- 
- 
-

## CAREER TOOLBOX—
## Performance Chart™

Jobs change. The longer you stay in an organization performing a specific job, the more change and adaptation the job is likely to go through. Duties assigned when you were hired five years ago might be very different from those you perform in the same position today. If you seek a promotion or a raise, you'll find the performance chart a good tool to use.

**Your job has increased in responsibility. Note the additions when asking for a raise or promotion.**

### THE TECHNIQUE

This chart compares the responsibility changes from the original job description to the new job duties and notes significant accomplishments achieved.

### PURPOSE

Using this tool will draw attention to the additional responsibilities and level of growth you've made on the job to support a request that your employer realign the job to reflect the actual (and higher) level of current responsibilities and performance.

### USES

1. Asking for a promotion, you can easily show the major difference between what you were originally hired to do and all the new duties you now perform. This chart clearly shows the extras often taken for granted by bosses simply because you've added them as they evolved over time.

2. This provides evidence when asking for a raise by basing the request on the fact that additional (or more advanced) responsibilities have been assigned, while neither salary nor title have been increased or changed to compensate for these additional contributions.

### EXAMPLES

Stephanie worked in the office administration area for a very large organization. Highly productive, she has many talents that she applied to her job. She'd been there two and a half years when a new boss took over the department. Within a couple months, the new boss called Stephanie into his office and praised her for all she was doing in her job. He noticed that she did a great deal more than her job originally indicated. He suggested she write a letter noting her original duties and include all the new activities she was currently doing. He'd support her, but she'd have do all the work herself and go through the union and proper personnel channels. Stephanie took the ball and created this chart to more clearly demonstrate she was now performing a higher-level job. She was thorough in the hopes of persuading her company to promote her.

It worked—she obtained a five-grade promotion and a $15,000 raise!

Note: Some jobs don't have a formal job description. In that case, simply create one, noting the original duties as you remember them plus state exactly what you are doing now.

## PERFORMANCE CHART™—STEPHANIE FIATERRY

| Old | New | Contributions |
|-----|-----|---------------|
| Serve as office clerk within department. | Maintains the computerized tracking systems for department. | Worked as department liaison with MIS to install an entirely new computer network system into department. |
| Provide the maintenance, compilation, preparation, and certification of claim records and reports. | Trains other staff on all computer systems; updates computer training manuals. | Trained staff managers on new system usage. |
| Type records and reports. | Coordinates software and systems modifications. Interacts with MIS for corporate networking integrations. | Coordinates all software usage and enhancements on system. |
| Talks with customers to obtain claim information. | Coordinates all invoicing and computerized billing. | Developed customized reports, budgeting spreadsheets, invoice and claim-tracking systems. |
| Prepares and verifies claims bills. | Generates reports. | Provide executive assistance to the division manager. |
| Types letters to customers on claim notification. | Provides secretarial support exclusively to the division manager, including calendar scheduling, travel arrangements, meeting coordination, and mail sorting. | |
| Files. | Provides project management. | |
| Needed skills: typing, adding machine, copying, fax. | | |

# Resumés, Cover Letters, and Other Career Arsenal Essentials

The focus of this book has been to influence the employer during the interview or performance meeting. I would be remiss if I did not point out three other components that are a vital part of your career arsenal:

*Resumés* are an advertisement to the world of your special skills and accomplishments. So important is a resumé that I've devoted an entire book (*Winning Resumés,* published by Wiley) to aid you in creating one that employers notice. To research that book I surveyed 600 hiring managers. In it you will find new and important insights into what employers want in a resumé. To impress them, you need to offer specific, concrete contributions. The important persuasion message your resumé must convey is that of how your actions have achieved specific results for past employers. To create a resumé employers notice, I highly recommend you use my book, *Winning Resumés.*

*Cover Letters* are important and necessary. Employers see them as an example of your written communication skills. My survey of 600 hiring managers provided specific insights and noted the numerous mistakes most job hunters make. My book, *Winning Cover Letters* (published by Wiley) is of tremendous assistance in writing powerful and influential cover letters employers notice. Both your resumé and cover letter lay the foundation for the persuasion techniques you'll use in the interview.

*Education* has become a necessary credential to get a career started and ensure your advancement. There's been a lot of debate about the importance of degrees. Many job hunters use numerous excuses for why that "little piece of paper" doesn't mean much. They can argue all they want about the importance of obtaining college degrees and specialty training, but the employer has the final say on this. *The bottom line is that employers value degrees and education.* Therefore, you'll need to obtain the appropriate degrees for your profession. If you do not, you may limit your career growth.

---

**CAREER TOOLBOX—**
- *Your Resumé*
- *Your Cover Letter*
- *Your Education*

---

**CAREER COACH** *fact*

**Department of Labor studies show that lifetime earnings increase with education:**

High school graduate will earn $821,000

Associate's degree will earn $1,062,000

Bachelor's degree will earn $1,421,000

Master's degree will earn $1,619,000

*MBAs and Other Graduate Degrees.*   Graduate school is a sacrifice. It often means working while attending classes at night or on weekends. Decisions about whether to go to business school, law school, or to enter other programs can get clouded by listening to others with good intentions. Here's a rule of thumb I've always used to advise clients about graduate school: Determine if *employers* deem it necessary to possess the degree to perform the job you wish to do. If the answer is yes, then select the best program to meet your needs and achieve your goal of obtaining that degree.

*Not a Meal Ticket.*   Degrees are a part of your career arsenal. They alone do not create or give you a career. They aid you in that they substantiate your experience with the foundation of formal education. An MBA from Harvard will land you a great first job, but if you fail miserably, your future will be more questionable. The combination of college degrees and/or specialty credentials *plus* your on-the-job performance will ensure your future.

## Delivering the Tools

Your persuasion tools can be outstanding, but unless you project confidence and competence you may not succeed. Always remember, no one knows how you feel inside—all they see is what you project outside. The delivery with which you conduct the interview or meeting will tremendously affect the outcome. The words you choose, the body language, the tone of your voice—all can add to your success or detract from it. The last part of your persuasion package is the delivery. An in-depth understanding of this powerful skill—delivery—will give you the edge in your communications with others.

### WORD SELECTION

In many of the tools, you see specific word choices. In the Salary Extractor, you respond to the employer's question about your salary requirements with the words, "What is the range this job pays?" Important, powerful words keep you in control of obtaining your goal—getting the job and as high a salary as possible. Each persuasion tool offers examples of words, phrases, and even scripts of what to say. Additionally, there are some words to avoid. These subtract from your presence and your strength.

These are phrases to *avoid:*

✔ *"I'll be honest with you."*   The underlying message here is that you were lying before.

✔ *"Frankly . . ."*   This also evokes suspicion.

✔ *Apologizing for things out of your control.*   If you are not guilty, don't apologize. Instead of saying, "I'm sorry the power went out during my presentation," which is a weak statement (after all, you didn't cause the power to go out), you would do better to say, "It was unfortunate that the power went out during my presentation. I plan to summarize the content and copy some of the overheads and get those out to everyone no later than tomorrow." Here you show the problem and solution—a stronger communication.

✔ *Sounding overconfident.*   An arrogant, self-aggrandizing tone can really irritate others. Don't say, "Naturally, you'll agree with my assessment that I deserve the raise." Instead say, "My assessment of my current job duties shows the additional tasks and responsibilities I've undertaken that warrant a salary increase." Men tend to make this mistake. There's a thin line between confidence and oversell. Strive to be professional, assured, and not the Kmart "Blue Light Special."

✔ *Appearing meek, mild, and weak.*   Confidence must be projected. Hesitant statements with downcast eyes (such as "Don't you think?") or a great deal of "ums" can detract from the strength of your request to persuade. Women, too often uncomfortable with their own value, are guilty of this. Other words that create a weaker message are "kind of," "sort of," "really," "you know."

✔ *Negative self-statements.*   Personal put-downs are always ineffective. Never say, "This is probably stupid, but . . ." or "I may be wrong."

✔ *Empty superlatives.*   "Terrific," "great," "fantastic," when overused or without sincerity, become meaningless.

Positive word choices can add to your effectiveness. Change today. Incorporate words and phrases that better illustrate your competence. Make these a daily habit:

✔ Use direct, positive statements (e.g., "I did," "I can").

✔ Use "I" and take credit for your accomplishments (e.g., "I reorganized the files and we saved two hours of time per week with the new, easier system").

✔ Select and use words that communicate your strengths and contributions (e.g., *created, developed, implemented, tested,* etc.).

✔ Practice.

## BODY LANGUAGE

There is hidden meaning in the way you stand, hold yourself, gesture, and in your voice tone and rate of speech.

## FACIAL EXPRESSIONS

Look into the mirror and make your face look nervous, scared, frightened. Now make your face appear happy, laughing. You can see the difference. So can your manager when you talk to her or him. Practice controlling the nervous face and put in place a relaxed, more happy one. Positive facial gestures are one of the keys to success.

**Nonverbal communication is a vital source of feedback on how well your message is getting across.**

## EYE CONTACT

Suspicion is quickly cast on the person who averts his or her eyes. You seem either fearful or untrustworthy. Try this out for yourself. Get a friend to look you in the eye and sincerely ask you for $20. Now get the same person to ask for $20, but have them tilt their head down and avert their eyes. Feel the difference? So do employers. Eye contact is a vital component to your delivery. Work hard to maintain it.

## POSTURE

Pulling away or leaning back from someone changes the energy. Downward movements or drooping shoulders transmit a negative message—discouraged, unable, weary, burned out. *Leaning into a conversation increases the energy and the connection to the person with whom you are speaking. Excellent posture denotes power and confidence.* Even if you feel depressed, straighten up, pull in your stomach, hold your head erect, and smile. The world will think you feel confident and wonderful. That's what actors do all the time—they project feelings or emotions. You must project confidence and belief in yourself and your abilities.

## HANDSHAKE

Develop a firm (but not bone-crushing) handshake. Always lean toward people as you shake their hand, nod slightly as you greet them, smile, and say their name. That makes a personal and powerful connection to start with or end with.

### SMILE

Nothing is more powerful than your smile. It warms your face and makes us want to believe and trust you more. Smiling during the interview shows confidence and poise.

### VOICE TONE

Vocal variety is the spice of life. It makes us interesting. Yet many people go into interviews or salary negotiations and become deadly serious, never smiling, using a monotone. Let me assure you from personal experience interviewing hundreds of job candidates, nothing causes an employer to tune out faster than a monotone job candidate. Boring the interviewer can put you out of the running. Be yourself. Use your voice to create different inflections and tones for interest and to make points. In other words, just be yourself and talk as you would in normal conversation. Show the employer you'd be a pleasant person to have in the office. Subtle, yes, but important nonetheless.

### SPEECH RATE

Nervousness usually causes people to babble, to speak too fast, or to speak too slowly. Fear can exaggerate the situation. Try to speak normally. Avoid adding to answers. Learn to tolerate silence as the employer or your manager absorbs what you've said and the points you've made. Work to keep the conversation moving along. Don't go too fast—they'll miss your points. Too slow and they'll lose the train of thought. A good rule of thumb is to follow the speed the other person sets.

## *Creating a Great First Impression*

*Style.* Nothing is harder to overcome than a poor first impression. When you walk into the interview, those first 30 seconds are critical—the employer must look at you and feel that you could be a good representative of their organization. Let's sneak inside these employers' offices and peak into the employers' initial thoughts as Cassie, Joan, Jolene, Frank, Tim, and Ken come in for job interviews.

**Position: Assistant program director**
**Applicant: Cassie Stonewall**

Jennifer, a Midwestern college program director, glanced over the resumé and was pleased with Cassie's (the applicant's) background. The institution could sure use the organizational computer skills listed. A knock at the door caused Jennifer to raise her head. There stood Cassie. She walked in and cordially shook Jennifer's hand. "I cannot believe it," Jennifer thought to herself. "That skirt is so short it barely extends beyond her blazer. The eyeliner looks like someone went crazy on Halloween. Ankle socks—when did they get popular? And that sexy, flowing hair—are those triple earrings? No, this will never work. She'll give students the wrong impression about us. My boss would kill me if I ever hired her. Okay—let's make this quick." Then she began and soon ended the interview.

**Position: Credit manager**
**Applicant: Joan King**

Bill, the company's controller, had already interviewed seven people for the job. The next one, Joan King, showed promise. She had 15 years at a Fortune 500 company—the type of experience his job needed. Bill's boss had inquired how the selection was going. "Be sure I get to meet the candidate before you extend the offer," his boss had said. "I've got to hire a great person," thought Bill, "especially with my boss watching over my shoulder."

Joan King was in her mid-50s, significantly overweight, and wore pasty make-up—bright lipstick with a poorly cropped haircut. The color, poorly dyed, was too dull and artificial-looking—not flattering to her skin tone. In just seconds as Bill saw her, his hopes deflated. "Frumpy, dowdy" were his first thoughts. "Old and rigid. Stern-looking, no handshake—she's one tough cookie and her suit doesn't fit; the blouse is pulling apart. I bet she's a hard one to get to change or be innovative. I think that second lady, Cathy, is the best one of the lot." The interview was then conducted, but it was all over 60 seconds after Joan walked in the door.

## Position: Director of corporate events
## Applicant: Jolene Cavanaugh

Mary was overworked, and finding the perfect person to head corporate events was proving to be a challenge. They needed savvy negotiation skills, tons of experience, and a proven track record. Plus they needed to have that "special something."

Mary looked up as Jolene walked into her office, smiling, hand extended in a warm greeting. "Terrific suit, and wow, what enthusiasm and panache," Mary thought. Jolene showed promise. Mary had not been at all put out by Jolene's gray hair or 62-year-old face. She was a contemporary woman who radiated vitality, not an old lady. Jolene had dressed carefully, selecting colors that would enhance her appearance. She had a flair for fashion, but was still conservative. Knowing the competition would be half her age, she kept the conversation focused on her new ideas and program development success in recent years. High energy and enthusiasm did the rest to create an instant rapport with Jolene's potential employer, Mary. Off to a great start, she sailed through the interviews, using her enthusiasm and persuasion techniques. Jolene got this job that nearly 300 others had also applied for.

## Position: Vice president
## Applicant: Frank Sherman

Ted, the company's CEO, waited for the next candidate to enter. Frank had spent the majority of his career with his current employer. He had solid industry experience. Ted eagerly waited to meet him. Frank walked in, a short man, 5 feet 6 inches, and at least 150 pounds overweight. He seemed to be slightly out of breath and very nervous. As he sat down, Ted thought, "I'm not impressed. Image is a substantial part of this job. He might not have the physical stamina for our job—the travel schedule, the long flights through multiple time zones. He seems out of breath and sluggish. He'll never keep up with our pace. What will our customers think as they sit across from him and stare at a giant white belly hanging over his suit pants? Seems like the resumé was the best thing about this guy. He'll have to be truly spectacular to change my opinion now. Let's get this over with so I can meet the next candidate." The next candidate got the job.

**Position: Manager**
**Applicant: Tim Blewsheed**

Deidre, the HR manager, got ready for a full day of initial interviews. She would screen out the poorer ones and refer the top four or five people on to the second interview. She sighed to herself as Tim walked in the door. "How can these people come to an interview as if they just rolled out of bed? The suit is so wrinkled, it's as if he gave no thought at all to the color coordination—suit, tie, and shirt—they're awful together. His hair is so greasy, it looks like he hasn't washed it in a week. Those shoes look like they've never been polished, and they are so worn out. Okay, here he comes—uck—I hate clammy palms and wimpy handshakes. Let's get this over with—oh dear— he's got on short socks—now that he's crossed his knees I'm staring at white flesh. I knew he wasn't our kind of employee. Nothing with him, no pen or notepad—he'll never make it here. We need them sharp, organized, and on top of things. He's a *no*."

**Position: Engineer**
**Applicant: Ken Marinetti**

Gordon, a hiring manager at Hewlett-Packard, looked up and was pleasantly surprised to see Ken in a suit—an expensive, great-looking one at that. "This guy's going places," he thought. Hewlett-Packard, like most computer companies, had a very informal dress code— mostly T-shirts, jeans, or Dockers. "Nice briefcase and great smile and handshake," thought Gordon. "Confident—I like that. This guy looks as good as his resumé—all right!" Ken smiled, and the interview began. Ken did land the job, plus a significantly higher salary than he currently had. Ken told me he *knew* he looked good, and that gave him more confidence. It helped—he got the job.

## It's Clothes and More

As you can see from these examples, a great deal of judgment happens in the mind of the employer. The right outfit does not assure you of the job. Very early in my career, I went to an interview in which a school district had four openings for certified vocational counselors. I bought a terrific suit and was overly self-assured—I did look terrific. The interview panel had a lot of technical and professional questions. My overconfidence came from the fact that few people held the same vocational certification I did. It was a real eye-opener when I called the employer back after the interview. I did *not* get the job. In fact, I'd done such a poor job answering the questions, they left two jobs *unfilled*. They would rather have *no one* than me—no one. That day, I learned two important things: The professional image was essential, but it was only the start of the persuasion process. Substance, researching the employer's needs, analyzing my skills, preparing answers to potential questions, developing my selling strategy—these were also vital to success. (Incidentally, I do learn from my mistakes. I've been *very* prepared for every interview I've had since this embarrassing day 14 years ago. Every interview I've gone to since has turned into a job offer.)

Being dressed professionally was, and is, just the first step. It's the nod the employer gives you toward acceptance—"yes, this person would be a good representative of us"—so that the employer will *continue* to evaluate you as a candidate. Mistakes can cause the employer to totally tune you out, which is exactly what happened to Cassie Stonewall, the miniskirt lady who wanted the assistant program director job.

Learn your lessons from this book—not through firsthand experience. The formula for success includes both a winning professional suit and the tools to persuade and convince the employer to hire *you.*

## The Professional, Impressive-Attire Formula

A human resources manager at a Fortune 500 company told me: "Our managers and executives dress very well here. We expect it. A candidate must project a positive, self-confident image to keep our attention as we interview potential employees."

### THE "LOOK OF SUCCESS" RECOMMENDATIONS FOR MEN

*Dark suit:* High quality, navy blue or deep gray, pinstripe or solid. Style—conservative. Excellent fit is imperative. If overweight, be sure to select a suit design that's slimming and covers protruding stomachs when sitting or standing.

*White shirt:* Oxford, professionally dry-cleaned, light starch for crispness.

*Conservative silk tie:* Dots, stripes, conservative pattern. Avoid all loud colors, Jerry Garcia–like images, or cutesy things such as Santa Clauses.

*Jewelry:* Dress watch, dark leather band. Nothing too clingy or gaudy. Wedding band if you're married. No earrings!

*Shoes:* Classic dress shoes, black or cordovan, freshly polished and in excellent condition. (Check soles; resole them if the heel is worn down.)

*Socks:* Over-the-calf, matched to suit color.

*Hair:* Contemporary, short, neatly trimmed, combed, and clean. Use a tiny bit of hair spray to hold in place. No gels, mousses, or pompadour hairdos.

*Coat:* Overcoat, dress coat, dark color or khaki. No ski parkas or short jackets. No leather.

*Fragrance:* Light cologne. Apply sparingly or use none at all. Good scents for business meetings: Tommy Hilfiger, Royal Copenhagen, Eternity (by Calvin Klein).

*Briefcase:* Notebook and pen. Use high-quality leather briefcase with color-coordinated leather notepad folder. Gold or other high-quality pen is a must.

*Nails:* Trimmed and clean.

*Other suggestions:*

1. Do not chew gum.
2. If you wear glasses, be sure they are in excellent condition and clean.
3. No casual reading—novels and magazines are best left at home or in your car.
4. Smile often; maintain solid eye contact.

## THE "LOOK OF SUCCESS" RECOMMENDATIONS FOR WOMEN

*Suit:* Conservative, high quality. Navy blue, black, beige, burgundy, or any color that you know you look great in. Recommend you use color and image consultant available at prominent department stores if you are uncertain what looks best on you. Contemporary style is essential, high fashion only for fashion-related jobs. Excellent fit is imperative—select style to diminish any figure flaws. Scarves and color near face draw away from rest of your silhouette.

*Dress option:* Coat dress, dark color. Be sure no slip shows. Most women do not look professional in floral-patterned dresses with simple, sloppy blazers—avoid. You want to achieve a tailored, crisp look.

*Skirt length:* At knee, below knee preferably. No more than 1 inch above knee.

*Blouse:* Cream, white, or matching silk shell. Buttoned in the back is a better alternative. Avoid sheer and lacy fabrics.

*Shoes:* Matched to suit color. High quality, leather, 1- to 2-inch heels, closed toe, polished and in good condition.

*Stockings:* Neutral color or matched to suit.

*Coat:* Winter, wool coat or long raincoat. No ski parkas, furs, or leather.

*Make-up:* Light, but make-up does enhance your features. Use complementary lipstick—neither extremely dark nor too bright a color. Make-up should enhance your face, not be the focal point. Be sure no make-up gets on your clothes or teeth.

*Fragrance:* Light, clean scent. Be careful to not overspray—you may not smell it, but others don't like to smell you from a room away. Good scents for business meetings: Eternity for Woman, Allure by Channel, White Linen by Estée Lauder, Wings by Georgio, Polo Sport by Ralph Lauren.

*Nails:* Manicured, clear, or newly polished nails (no chips). Avoid dragon lengths, multicolor, or designs.

*Hair:* Contemporary style, light spray. Freshly washed looks best. Long hair should be pulled back with stylish, clipped ponytail, or put up in a French braid. Avoid evening or sexy looks. Don't use excessive mousse, gels, or sprays. No ridged, cement-poofy, old-fashioned styles. An updated hairstyle does wonders to take years off your face. Avoid keeping the college look into your 30s. A sophisticated hairdo is much more impressive.

*Purse and briefcase options:* Do not have a cluttered look. A big purse, a briefcase, and a notebook in your hands presents a disorganized image. Try one of these:

1. Put a small purse inside your briefcase.
2. Carry a small purse and a leather notepad holder.
   Include a leather notepad and high-quality or gold pen for taking notes.

*Jewelry:* Nice watch, gold or silver earrings, not dangly. Simple gold chain or a pin. Be conservative in your selection. Less is better. Nothing gaudy.

*Other suggestions:*

1. Do not chew gum.
2. If you wear glasses, be sure they are in excellent condition and clean.

3. No casual reading—novels and magazines are best left at home or in your car.
4. Smile often; maintain solid eye contact.
5. Camouflage a weight problem with a contemporary, dark suit—must fit well; select a cut that tends to slenderize.

## Remaining Professional in a Casual World

Companies are going casual, relaxing dress codes all across America. "The irony," says Lisa Bayne, a vice president at Eddie Bauer, "is that companies have moved to casual dress codes to make people more comfortable and at ease. But until both employees and managers understand exactly what is meant by 'casual,' there is a great deal of discomfort and people feeling ill at ease. Casual wear varies from city to city and company to company. Unlike traditional business attire—the suit—casual wear cannot be so simply defined."

If you are on the fast track to getting a promotion, you need to give some serious thought to exactly what style you want to emulate on a daily basis.

You need to be sensible and consistent in your choices. Mistakes in dress can derail your career as upper management glances over the ranks.

**Sloppy and too-casual attire can hurt your career.**

### BEWARE OF MAJOR MISTAKES, FAUX PAS AND OTHER CAREER EMBARRASSMENTS

Darlene had come to work at her managerial position at a Fortune 100 company on Monday in her normal casual attire, a silk blouse and a nice, tailored pair of dress pants. She opened her daily calendar and was shocked to find that the meeting for the 12 United Way Coordinators (of whom she was one) with the company's CEO was in one hour. She looked okay, but if she had remembered, she would have worn a suit. As she entered the CEO's office, Darlene scolded herself for wearing her casual clothes and forgetting. The room was impressive, with a spectacular city view, and she shook hands with the CEO for the very first time.

Thirty minutes later (15 minutes after the event began), Betty walked in dressed in stretch pants and a stretched-out, baggy old sweater. She said out loud to the group: "I'm sorry I'm late. I forgot about this or I would have dressed up." She made a poor impression on every person in the room. Two major faux pas: (1) being late for the CEO reception honor-

**CAREER COACH** *tip*

*Never dress so casually that a surprise visit to a client or top management would require an explanation or apology.*

ing the 12 selected people (which might have been overlooked) and (2) *bringing attention* to her unprofessional appearance. These types of mistakes can kill a career.

Bill was an attorney whose company had a "casual Friday" policy. He wore Dockers and a long-sleeved polo shirt with sneakers to work. Something unexpected came up, and he had to visit a client whose office was full of men in suits and ties. The client commented about not understanding "this casual Friday stuff," and Bill was put in a difficult and embarrassing predicament as he explained some technical legal point in his Dockers and polo.

### CASUAL DRESS FOR THE FAST TRACK TO MAINTAIN A PROFESSIONAL IMAGE

Exercise common sense when selecting your work wardrobe. Here's a list of dos and don'ts and guidelines to help you remain professional.

✔ Follow the company's dress code.

✔ Notice both your boss and his or her manager's style of dress. Emulate and dress to their level unless the boss has no fashion sense. Select other managers and copy their leads.

✔ Dress appropriately. Never wear sexy clothing, jeans with holes, or inappropriate messages on T-shirts.

✔ Be prepared to upgrade if an important meeting or event comes up unexpectedly. Men should have a dress shirt, tie, and/or sports coat available to use in a pinch. Women should have a blazer and shell they could slip into.

✔ Listen to coworkers. If they think (or you feel) you're dressed too casually, then you are.

✔ Always dress up to deal with customers or clients.

✔ Wear clothes that fit.

✔ Avoid high fashion and trendy looks. Miniskirts are never appropriate for work.

✔ Be aware of the message you send forth. *Sloppy* may feel great, but may give the impression you are *disorganized* and not "move-up" material.

**CAREER COACH** *tip*

*Dress and act as if you already have the promotion and are performing at that level.*

# *Summary*

The persuasion tools are a mandatory part of your career arsenal. They provide the supplementary evidence so your words and delivery express confidence and belief in what you are saying. These tools can be easily adapted and used in your situation to achieve the career success you are after. As you see how these tools are used in the next few chapters, you'll begin to easily adapt them as a permanent part of your career arsenal. Employers will notice and remember you. Your message will be listened to. Raises, promotions, and new jobs will always be within your grasp. These tools help to advertise the very best about you. And employers will pay attention.

## Summary

# THE BEST WAYS TO LAND A GREAT JOB

## SUCCESS

*If I wanted to become a failure
I would seek advice from men
who have never succeeded.*
*If I wanted to succeed in all
things, I would look around me
for those who are succeeding,
and do as they have done.*
—*JOSEPH MARSHALL WADE*

Y ou are unique. You have special talents and abilities to offer an employer. You take pride in your work and strive to do the best job possible. Recognize the fact that there is only one YOU!

No one else is quite like you. When you recognize you are unique and special, you begin to perceive yourself in a brighter light.

Let me give you an example. I am holding a glass of tap water. It is just plain old water out of the kitchen faucet. You are holding a bottle of Evian water. It cost about $1.79—it's just water, yet millions of people *buy* it. They perceive that Evian will taste better and therefore are willing to pay more for it. Evian sold $150 million dollars worth of bottled water last year because people believed it to be of higher value.

**Employers pay more for employees they place a higher value on.**

*Perceived value* is the value placed on something or someone according to what others perceive to be true. You must begin to see yourself as a bottle of Evian. To land a better job or obtain a raise, you must operate from the belief that you, as a worker, are offering great value for your services, just as Evian is perceived to be better than tap water. You must see yourself as a bottle of Evian.

Michael walked into my counseling room and had a look in his eyes that I had become familiar with. The pain in his eyes told me that Michael had lost his position. When men lose a job, it's a loss of identity. As a controller, Michael had spent nine years with his employer. A merger at the parent company about a year ago was responsible for the politics that resulted in his termination.

Michael told me what he'd done since his departure nearly seven months ago. The resumés he'd sent produced no interviews, and he had that feeling of desperation that crops up for many unemployed job hunters. The executive recruiter hadn't been helpful. A referral from the CPA Society where I taught a lot of seminars brought Michael to me. He quickly realized that he had not been using the most effective tools to look for a job. We created a new resumé and more effective cover letters. Then I taught Michael all about the "hidden job market." He was astounded to find that the want ads and recruiters were not the only ways to find a job.

**Labor studies reveal that 85% of all jobs are never advertised.**

Michael left with an action plan and three months later wrote to say, "I had to tell you I found an exceptionally good job. It was never advertised—'hidden,' like you said. The company is in an exciting growth phase, and when I used all your tools I landed the job and an $8,000 raise. This success is a direct result of using your highly effective methods."

There are many strategies that you can use to get an employer to call you in for an interview. In this chapter, I've outlined the more common, as well as set forth the most effective. I recommend you adopt most, if not all, of the hidden job market techniques. These will help you uncover the truly outstanding jobs. Create your job search action plan utilizing several of these techniques and you'll quickly move into the persuasion phase. Our goal here is to uncover great jobs—interesting and appealing ones that you can get excited about. Don't hold yourself back. You can go after that dream job. These techniques will help you meet employers, talk to hiring managers, and do what Michael did—find an exceptional job.

## The Want Ads

Michael was a perfect example of most job hunters: They need a crash course on what works in today's competitive marketplace. Michael answered over 100 ads, many of which he was either overqualified or underqualified to do. He'd done no market research. He used a shotgun approach. He waited until Sunday and spent many hours of wasted effort applying for jobs that did not match his qualifications.

Want ad competition is steep. A classified ad in the Sunday paper can produce 200 to 400 resumés in response. To save time and effort, follow this rule of thumb: In a competitive marketplace respond to an ad only if you have most of the skills the employer is requesting. If employers want eight years' experience and you have three, it's very remote that they'll select you from the competition, at least several of whom will have the requested eight years of experience.

A lot of people apply for jobs they aren't qualified for. A client once asked me to help with a cover letter for the job of director of student services for a local community college. I looked through the job description and asked her, "Do you have any program management experience? Have you supervised student programs before? Do you have a minimum of five years of college experience?" She said no to each question, yet those were the three major requirements for performing this job. She did add, "But I know I could do it." Maybe she could. But once the employer has put an ad in the newspapers, hundreds will apply. Certainly a few dozen will have done the exact job the employer is recruiting for. Sometimes you can stretch a little bit, but if you're not even in the ballpark, don't waste your time writing cover letters and sending out resumés for jobs that are not a solid match. When responding to a want ad, the secrets for moving to the top of the employer's stack of candidates are as follows:

> ## WANT AD SUCCESS SECRETS
>
> 1. **Apply for only those jobs you are adequately qualified for.**
> 2. **Write a targeted cover letter using the Power Impact Technique. (This has a powerful opening sentence and is taught with numerous examples and employers' insights in my book *Winning Cover Letters,* published by Wiley.)**
> 3. **When possible, call to request a copy of the complete job description.**
> 4. **Use contacts and colleagues to provide insider information on the employer's true needs and concerns about performing the available job.**
> 5. **Contact employers directly for more information on their needs.**

The want ad is often an abridged version of what is actually desired. Affirmative Action requirements and personnel agendas can clutter up the ad. Sometimes, to keep costs down, virtually no information is listed. The more you know about the job needs, the easier it will be to target your skills and get the employer's attention.

## *Human Resources*

A common mistake that many job hunters make is to send their resumés to dozens of companies' *personnel offices.* Human resources' role is to screen people *out.* Unless there is a job opening (or a potential opening is coming up), your resumé is "held" for an indefinite amount of time, never to be seen again. In some offices your resumé is simply thrown out. Either way, it does not produce an interview or a job because personnel *does not hire* (except in its own area for its own human resources staff).

Personnel can provide an excellent overview of the company, its organizational structure, general job duties, and salary/benefit information. You don't need to waste your time contacting a lot of human resources offices. There are more effective ways that actually put you in front of your potential boss. I'll outline these shortly.

## Job Lines

Clients and seminar participants continue to affirm my long-held belief that calling job lines and listening to 45 minutes of unrelated openings is an enormous time waster. It's not productive, nor is it effective. A faster way to find out about openings is to ask personnel directly or call the department you're interested in and ask someone there. You can utilize the time saved to gather some information and write a better and more effective cover letter.

## Mass Mailings

A common technique that many outplacement firms recommend involves sending a hard-sell letter to 100 or more organizations, firms, or companies. It's a way to survey a large segment of a given field, to generate job leads, or to target a new geographical area. However, mass mailings are one of the least effective ways of finding a job, producing less than a 3% return. That means for every 100 letters you send out, you'll receive only about three responses, and that doesn't necessarily mean three interviews. Some of the responses will be rejections.

People try mass mailings in the hope that by blanketing a large number of employers they might get lucky and "hit" something. These letters are typically sent to personnel departments, which quickly disregard them.

Victor, a CEO, shared this insight with me: "One of the worst mistakes job hunters make is mailing out those obvious form letters to find a job. It's never targeted to me or my company's needs. It's a general approach that's unimpressive and ineffective at best."

# Cold Calls

*Cold calling* is a sales technique often used in job hunting. You telephone or drop in to see an employer in the hope of connecting with the person who has the power to hire you. You try to make connections, obtain leads, and get a firsthand view of the company. Cold calls work best when your energy is high, as this technique meets with a great deal of rejection. Practice your communication skills and your opening lines. Your 60 Second Sell (Chapter 4, pp. 57–59) is crucial here. Confine each day's cold calls to one geographic area to save time and energy. Dress well and bring along copies of your resumé and references.

A major downside to cold calling is that it's time-consuming. It's also frustrating—there is a very high rate of rejection. Results are often not effective. It's a technique that works best when looking for a retail position. You go to the mall and simply go from store to store asking if the manager is in and requesting a job application. Avoid busy times. If you are lucky and catch a manager who has time to talk to you, be prepared to sell yourself on the spot. But you probably won't see the person who has the power to hire you because he or she is usually too busy. Follow-up will be key.

# Temporary Work

Temporary work allows you to gain valuable work experience. It gives you a chance to get inside a company and find out about positions you may be qualified for. Almost all companies use temporary workers from time to time. Many highly skilled professionals sell their services as secretaries, receptionists, bookkeepers, salespeople, or word processors to earn income while they're looking for full-time employment. The trend for the next decade shows increasing use of professional temporary workers; employers will call and order an accountant for the day, or a public relations specialist, manager, or trainer to take on or complete a project. Engineers, programmers, and systems analysts may be paid by a temp agency but spend every workday on the job inside a major company. Manufacturers and large companies commonly fill their ranks with professional contract workers (another name for nonpermanent employees). Temporary work is a great way to learn about specific companies, and it gives you an inside edge to permanent work.

Many secretarial and clerical positions are found through temporary work. You go to work as a temporary, they like you, and you get hired on a full-time basis. Temporary agencies typically will charge the hiring employer a placement fee, often $500 to $700. This is much less than the fee ordinarily charged by employment agencies, which is one-third of your annual salary. Once an employer has tried you out and believes that you are a good fit, the employer is happy to pay the smaller fee and eliminate the hassle of filling a position through the traditional avenue of newspaper advertising. Many new college graduates or women reentering the workplace land their first "real" job starting as a temp.

Approach temporary work situations with a success strategy. Tell the temporary agency the companies where you want to work. Bring examples of your work, references, and a detailed resumé that describes the skills and the abilities you can sell through the temporary agency. Although you may be selling secretarial skills through the agency, once you are inside the company you may learn of other openings, and your new supervisor might be helpful in passing your resumé along to the right person. Do your research regarding temporary agencies and develop a relationship to ensure you will be placed in the kinds of jobs you want. Dress well—this is a job interview, and your appearance will affect whether the agency sends you out for work. If your performance is good on the first few assignments, that will guarantee a lot of future work with the agency. Experience, exposure, and job leads are the positive results of doing temporary work, and it helps pay the bills when your job search is extended or you find yourself unemployed. Many people find temporary work to be a hiring "back door." So explore it as a potential option.

## Employment Agencies

Agencies charge high fees to either you or the employer. Primarily, their job is to fill the openings that employers will pay for. Common in the legal, secretarial, and technical fields, this is a passive way to look for a job. Lots of people have horror stories about their terrible experiences with employment agencies. Do your homework. Check out the agency, its reputation, and its track record for success. Be very cautious before you sign any contract—read it carefully and understand exactly what costs or fees you will be responsible for.

# *Executive Recruiters*

Most recruiters specialize in a particular field and *work for the employer* to find an exact match for the employer's needs. Their services place middle and senior executives, plus CEOs, presidents, CFOs, and numerous specialty positions. Recruiters are in the "hot" fields where employer demand creates a need for their services. They service a small, elite group of job hunters, but if you offer the needed expertise they can be a resource you'd want to utilize.

Jennifer Lynch, a founding partner in one of Boston's most prominent executive recruiting firms, Kingston Dwight, offered these insights, "Recruiters work collaboratively with a candidate, but they need the real story. The person needs to be coachable and willing to listen to advice concerning the recruiter's client and the job search approach."

The recruiter can be a good source of insider information to aid you in developing your persuasion tools (60 Second Sell and 5 Point Agenda, Chapter 4). Recruiters can provide insight on current hiring and new business trends in the field. They are quite knowledgeable about the potential salary range for specific jobs and employers in their geographical area.

Today's marketplace changes so quickly that a new breed of employer is now expanding the executive recruiter's role in the hiring process. "In the Northeast," says Lynch, "we've seen a significant growth fueled by technology demands. The emergence of smaller high-tech companies—software, computer, telecommunications, biotech, Internet-related—needing employees has created a big market as those companies prefer to outsource the role of hiring. It's always the marketplace that creates the demand that recruiters hope to fill."

It makes no difference whether you are currently employed—it is the skill set and experience that makes you appealing to recruiters. If you wish to find a recruiter as one of your job-hunting strategies (don't abdicate the entire process to someone else or you may never find a new job) then follow these guidelines.

## GUIDELINES FOR USING A RECRUITER

- Identify well-respected recruiters by asking colleagues and senior executives for referrals. A referral will pique the recruiter's attention more than just a cold call from you alone.

- Identify two or three companies you're interested in. Call their human resources departments and ask for the names of executive recruiter firms and individuals they work with. This is a particularly helpful technique when you are seeking to relocate to a new city and may be completely unaware of who's who in that marketplace.

- Review professional trade journals and notice the employment ads and the recruiting firms that are placing them. Call and ask to speak to the individual who deals with your specialty or who placed the ad you noticed.

# *Beware of Scams*

This ad appeared in the *Seattle Times*:

**POLLUTION CONTROL**
**$30,000**
**ENTRY LEVEL**

BA/BS required. Responsible for monitoring water, air, land pollution. Assist in developing pollution prevention systems. Benefits. Job 100.

Employment Listing Service     Fee $120

No legitimate employer requires you to pay money to apply for a job. Too often, these deceitful ads are scams designed to rip you off. Therefore, *be very cautious* about the following:

✔ Ads that promise huge salaries and few work hours (most are multi-level marketing programs with large dollar investments required to "launch your business").

✔ Consultants/firms that charge exorbitant fees ($2,500 to $10,000) to find you a job. They play on your vulnerability by claiming "we've got all the contacts" or "you don't need to do anything—we'll do it." The fine print in their contracts never guarantees you a job. These firms often have many lawsuits against them from unsatisfied and still-unemployed customers. *Money* magazine recently identified this type of employment scam as the number one consumer rip-off in America. No one cares as much as you do about your finding a job. Use only certified/reputable career counselors who charge an hourly fee.

✔ Never pay to receive complete "job information," as in the preceding ad.

✔ Never pay a subscriber fee to electronic databases, resumé services, or job banks until you've seen firsthand the quality of the product. Inquire how current the listings are. Get references in your field who have used the services effectively. Many associations offer resumé services (databases or mailing services employers can use when recruiting for a new job) that are reputable and nominally priced or even free to members.

## *Job Hunting Strategies*

**MOST *COMMON* JOB HUNTING TECHNIQUES**

✔ Want ads—less than 10% of all jobs available.

✔ Executive Recruiters/Employment Agencies—never work for you.

✔ Personnel—function is to screen, not hire.

**MOST *EFFECTIVE* JOB HUNTING TECHNIQUES**

✔ Job Market Research

✔ Targeted Mailings

✔ Referral Campaign

✔ Networking

✔ Informational Interviewing

✔ Hiring Chart

**MOST *POTENTIAL* JOB HUNTING TECHNIQUES**

✔ Internet

## *Uncovering the Hidden Job Market*

For a few minutes, let's step inside Cynthia Richerman's office. She's director of engineering for a large manufacturer. Cynthia has just learned that one of her best project managers is leaving. With all the work on their plates, this is a big problem that Cynthia needs to solve ASAP. Let's peek inside Cynthia's head to get a firsthand glimpse of what a hiring manager is thinking and doing when faced with the need to add a new employee.

"Terrific," thinks Cynthia sarcastically, "he couldn't pick a better time to quit. I'm plowed over with work, and now I'll need to pick up some extra workload. Kathleen and Daniel will need to put in overtime—we can't let the process systems project get behind." Exasperated, she lets out a long breath. "Okay—got to hire someone," she resigns herself to the news. "Let me get out that file with those people who've sent me resumés recently. Hmmm," she ponders. "There's no one terrific here who could step in and fill Joe's shoes. I need to see if anyone else knows of someone who can help us."

A few hours later Cynthia calls a staff meeting. She addresses her staff: "Well, by now I'm sure you've heard Joe is moving on to a new city and job. I'm glad for him, but it will be a challenge for us to replace him. That's why I called you in here. Time is of the essence. You know that if I have to go through personnel it'll take three or four months to replace Joe. I want to speed that up and get someone on line in the next few weeks if at all possible. We can't get behind now. Several of you will need to pitch in until someone new is on board. Here's what would help: Please take some time and think of anyone who might be good for the job. You're all really familiar with the types of duties and skills we need a project manager to have. Call anyone who's good and have them fax a resumé and letter directly to me. Here's a memo you can send out that outlines the job. Off the top of your head, can anyone think of someone?" The staff people nod, no names are offered. "Okay," Cynthia says, "everybody, let's work on this—top priority."

Cynthia heads back to her office, where she finds a message from Kent, who's been working with her on an engineering association committee. When she calls him back, she quickly tells him, "We're looking for a new project manager, Kent—do you happen to know of anyone we should consider?" Kent says, "No, not at this time." Cynthia calls a dozen colleagues over the next few days. "I've got to get someone good," she says, feeling powerless to make the perfect project manager appear at her door.

At the start of the next week, Cynthia passes out her job-opening memo at a department-head meeting and sends it to the company's internal job listing service. After four weeks and three or four people who just weren't right, she sends the opening to personnel.

Three weeks later the ad appears in the Sunday newspaper. It's another four weeks before personnel finally calls Cynthia to look at the 20 resumés they've sorted out from the 413 they received. It takes another four weeks for interviews and then two more weeks to get the new person on board. Cynthia is exhausted. She sits in her office reviewing the whole process. "I hate hiring," she thinks. "I've got so much to do, and it takes so much time. Over four months I've clocked in nearly 200 extra hours between the work and the hiring stuff. I hope this new woman works out. I wish someone I knew had recommended her. I hope no one ever, ever quits again."

Cynthia is typical of most hiring managers. They find the entire process trying and somewhat exasperating.

She also points out the two major reasons why the hidden market exists:

**63% of people hired in the last year were found through contacts.**

1. Time

2. Better employee fit

Once the bosses know they need a new employee, they want to hire someone fast to get on with the work. They also want someone "good." When asking for referrals, it is hoped that the person asked (assumed to be more familiar with the organization and job) will recommend a better potential employee. These two factors keep the hidden job market alive, well, and an active part of America's employment process.

I want you to begin to concentrate your efforts on the *hidden job market,* since most of the better jobs are found there. You've completed Chapter 3, "Define Your Best Skills and Ideal Job." That assessment has helped create a clearer job target and focus for you. You need to know exactly what you are looking for so that these techniques can maximize your success.

Figure 5.1 graphically outlines exactly how the hiring process works, starting with the manager's need to hire someone. The normal process is

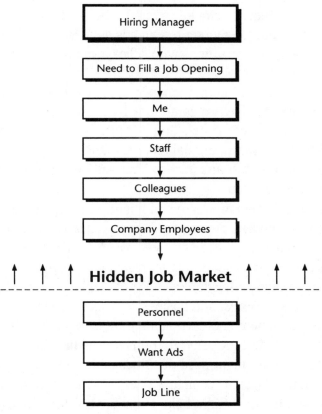

**Figure 5.1** The Hiring Process

for managers to review their own records, ask staff, and call colleagues. These are people they network with and trust. The *hidden job market* refers to the window of time before the position has been formally advertised in the newspapers. This is when you want to place yourself in front of the employer, since that's how most jobs get filled, especially in new and emerging fields and high-tech industries. The upcoming techniques show you how.

Once you begin to tap into the hidden job market, you'll be excited and full of hope that a bright and better future is just ahead.

## Job Market Research

Approximately 85% of all jobs are not advertised. I've found that the best way to achieve personal career satisfaction is to work for an organization you like and respect. This technique allows you to sort through potential organizations that meet your ideal company profile (see Chapter 3, pp. 36–54).

The purpose of job market research is to uncover leads for potential jobs, names of prospective employers, and sources of information to aid you in your job hunt. Job market research is done in the library, over telephones, by having conversations with colleagues and associates, or on the Internet.

Abundant sources of information exist, but probably the best place to start is the library. A reference librarian will be most helpful in your job search: They can help you access fingertip information with amazing speed. Business directories, annual reports, CD-ROM databases of employers, trade journals, and publications—all hold gold mines of potential job leads for you.

The kind of information you're seeking includes names, addresses, phone numbers, and lists of companies or organizations. Your sources are trade journals, business directories, newspapers, magazines, even the Yellow Pages. One publication I highly recommend is your local business journal. In most cities, it has ranked a list of employers by fields, including new products, services, and business changes. Whenever you read about a new store opening or a company that is expanding into a new service area, draw the conclusion that this means new jobs. Make note of any organization that might need the kinds of services you can provide. Record information such as company size, growth potential, name of the manager—anything that might help you make contact with the employer.

Any company that's publicly traded on the stock market has an annual report that you can receive by calling company headquarters and asking that it be sent to you. Or check the company's web site. Many annual reports can now be seen online. Annual reports contain valuable information on company growth, new products and services, plus new regional offices that are planned and the names of top management.

Professional associations are a great source of information. Often they have a directory that lists companies or organizations along with the names and phone numbers of people who work there. The association's directory is a very underused, but valuable, resource.

You can make contacts by attending meetings or annual conferences. An association can provide excellent career information about the field, types of jobs, salary ranges, where people are getting hired, and future trends. Association newsletters often have articles about people in the profession, and they help keep you up-to-date on current jargon. For example, a marketing director working in the computer software industry might wish to make a career change to the food processing field. Such a person would need to conduct extensive market research, perhaps joining one or more associations to expand his or her knowledge of the special skills needed in the new industry. Conducting informational interviews with association officers is always a good place to start, since they are usually very knowledgeable about the field, and part of being an officer involves helping members (and potential members). They can become valuable contacts.

## Job Market Resource List

The following resources are available at public and college libraries and online libraries via the Internet:

*National Directory of Address and Telephone Numbers.*   Includes all SEC-registered companies, major law and accounting firms, banks, financial institutions, security dealers, consultants, advertising agencies, federal/state government offices, newspapers, radio stations, cable TV services/operators, media, periodicals by category, executive offices of hotel/motel chains. An extensive resource.

*Encyclopedia of Associations.*   Lists 22,000 active U.S. organizations. Also Includes *Regional, State, and Local Organizations.*

*Standard & Poor's Register of Corporations, Directors, and Executives.*   Lists 55,000 corporations, with thumbnail sketches on key executives.

*Dunn & Bradstreet's Million Dollar Directory.*   Excellent resource.

*Directories in Print.*   Descriptive guide to print and nonprint directories with e-mail and World Wide Web addresses; 15,096 listings indexed by title, keyword, or subject.

*Annual Reports*

*Consultants & Consulting Organizations Directory.*   Over 15,000 firms, individuals, and organizations.

*Contacts Influential.*   Business, commerce, industry areas listed by name, type, key personnel, etc.

*Macmillan's Directory of Leading Private Companies*

*Moody's Manual.*   Bank and finance, industrials, transportation, municipals, governments, public utilities, over-the-counter securities dealers.

*Business Organizations, Agencies and Publications Directories.* Lists 24,000 entries, including federal government, advisory organizations, newsletters, research services.

*Thomas' Register of American Manufacturers.*   Over 150,000 companies listed. Also available by state.

*Encyclopedia of Business Information Sources*

*Directory of American Firms Operating in Foreign Countries.*   Three volumes locating over 3,200 U.S. companies operating in more than 120 countries.

*Ward's Business Directory.*   Six volumes, Updated yearly. Covers 132,500 publicly and privately held companies.

*Government Job Finder.*   By Daniel Lauber. Thorough, with over 1,600 listings.

*Professional's Job Finder.*   By Daniel Lauber. Includes 2,500 listings.

*Nonprofits and Education Job Finder.*   By Daniel Lauber. Includes 1,350 listings.

*Fortune Magazine's 500 List Edition.*   Full of information on the biggest U.S. companies.

*Hoover's Handbook of American Business.*   Very good overview on 755 of the US's top companies.

*Hoover's Top 2,500 Employers.*   Brief listing by state.

*The Career Guide: Dun's Employment Opportunities Directory.* Outlines employers' potential hiring needs for over 5,000 U.S. companies.

*Job Seeker's Guide to Private and Public Companies.*   By Gale Research. Covers the basics on 17,000+ organizations. Four regional volumes.

*Dunn & Bradstreet's Reference Book.*   Good source of brief information on senior management.

*Infotrac.*   Database of newspaper, magazine, and trade journal articles over the previous four years.

*Almanac of American Employers.*   Annual edition includes 500 of the largest, fastest-growing U.S. employers.

*Directory of Executive Recruiters.*   Profiles of over 5,500 search firms in 2,200 locations.

*Occupational Outlook Handbook.*   U.S. Bureau of Labor Statistics brief overview of hundreds of jobs, covering duties, training required, average salary, and hiring outlook.

There are other library resources that can be helpful. Take time to read the last six to eight months of trade journals in your field, plus magazine articles that come to your attention. Scan the economic news in newspapers. Go back several months, because often there are announcements of new developments and opportunities. You won't find a directory or an article that says "New Job Openings in the Hidden Job Market." You need to sharpen your detective skills by spending a few hours in the library and a few hours with professional journals to develop your list of potential employers to contact.

Your goal is to develop a list of no less than 30 potential employers. Start creating your list on the "Employer Prospects" worksheet that follows. Too often, a job hunter has only one or two possibilities, and when these prospects fall through, it can be devastating. Knowing you have 30, 40, or even 50 other prospective employers will soften the blow when one turns you down. Job market research is not something you do once and forget about. It's an ongoing effort throughout your job search. If you run out of leads, go back to the library and continue your research. Pour through magazines, journals, the Yellow Pages, and old newspapers. Check old copies of the *National Business Employment Weekly.* Continue to add to your market research, to explore more companies to discover organizations that fit your ideal profile. Look for places where you think you'll really fit into the corporate culture because you are interested in the product, service, and mission of the company.

## EMPLOYER PROSPECTS

| Company | Address | Contact Person | Phone or E-mail | Action | Notes |
|---------|---------|----------------|-----------------|--------|-------|
|         |         |                |                 |        |       |
|         |         |                |                 |        |       |
|         |         |                |                 |        |       |
|         |         |                |                 |        |       |
|         |         |                |                 |        |       |
|         |         |                |                 |        |       |
|         |         |                |                 |        |       |
|         |         |                |                 |        |       |
|         |         |                |                 |        |       |
|         |         |                |                 |        |       |
|         |         |                |                 |        |       |
|         |         |                |                 |        |       |
|         |         |                |                 |        |       |

## Targeted Mailings

Self-marketing letters sent to targeted, specific employers and properly followed up can open some impressive doors to future job options. One retail buyer who had been "downsized" used this technique to get interviews with the head buyer for Macy's, Bloomingdale's, and Lord & Taylor when all her efforts through personnel yielded a big fat zero.

This approach focuses on obtaining accurate information such as names, titles, and addresses so you can mail your resume and cover letter to the person with the power to hire you. A quick phone call can identify the correct person to address your letter, and it can also weed out companies or organizations that don't have an appropriate job or division. For instance, some positions may exist only at company headquarters and not at regional offices where you may live.

Target mailings allow you to blanket a geographical area in a short time to learn which areas may be hot and which locations generate no leads. One of my clients, Paula, used this technique to help make a relocation decision. She was a lawyer, just finishing her degree, and wished to work in a law firm for a few years before deciding whether to open up her own practice. After researching and investigating several locations, she and her husband selected five cities to consider. The Yellow Pages from those cities produced a list of 700 firms. They mailed 700 targeted letters to the firms' partners, which yielded 21 responses. In a couple of her selected cities she got no response at all. One attorney even wrote, "Things are terrible here. The economy is bad and we're going through a recession. Several large employers have recently relocated out of the city." The advice was to pick a new location; now was not a good time to get a job or try to set up practice there.

Paula did receive nine responses from one of the selected cities. From them, she was able to arrange six interviews. Paula spent a week interviewing and was offered a job. During the week she spent in the new city, she and her husband decided they liked the area, so they made the move. Interestingly, as she continued to investigate the region, Paula heard about other positions and ended up working for a different law firm than the one that had made the original job offer.

Paula's plan worked because it was targeted to partners (the hiring managers) at the correct organizations (law firms). She asked people to respond if they had any interest because she wanted to pare down the five-city scope of her relocation project. She called every response, and that led to her visit to Atlanta, where she eventually took the job. Paula's approach worked for her, and it can yield results for you. It can be a good option to use if you plan to relocate and want to consider several different cities.

An even more effective way is to mail to a small, well-researched group of employers. This is easier to do when you live in the region where you seek a job. You select a handful of employers to begin with. You investigate their organizations and determine the correct person to contact. Your letter is targeted and laced with your top abilities—an introduction that includes a resumé. You mention you'll call in a few days. Then you do so. Here's where your persuasion skills come in handy. You open the conversation by stating who you are and inquiring whether they have received your letter. You ease into a 60 second pitch that includes your background and ask what their current needs are. If the hiring manager starts to chat—*bingo*—you may have a prospect. If he or she says, "We aren't hiring," take a moment to see if you can turn it into a job lead. Say, "I understand that. Maybe you can still help me out. Do you know of anyone who might be needing a [your job title] that has my experience?" This can often lead to a new name or two, and you're off and running.

Be persistent with your follow-up call. Don't give up until you actually speak to the hiring manager. Avoid leaving a message—you don't want an employer calling back and catching you off guard and unprepared. Good times to try are before 8 A.M., immediately after 5 P.M., and during lunch, when you can often catch hiring managers at their desks answering their own phones.

Conversations with hiring managers can and do lead to information about potential openings. Michelle sent a dozen letters over a four-week period. She had a particularly difficult time reaching one manager. She called numerous times (but didn't leave her name). Finally, they connected. Someone had just quit and she was invited in for an interview. Three days later, she started as the new executive account representative, with a company car and high base salary that also included a lucrative commission structure.

## TARGETED MAILINGS SUCCESS SECRETS

✔ Create a targeted letter that specifically identifies the job you seek and summarizes your strongest skills to perform that job.

✔ Mail the letter with a resumé directly to the department head or hiring manager.

✔ State in the letter you'll contact them in a few days to learn more about their current needs.

✔ Make the follow-up call. Don't leave a message. Instead, continue to call until you reach the manager. If you get a secretary, ask for a good time to reach the person.

✔ Try to obtain a referral if no opportunities exist at this organization.

✔ In large companies, ask for referrals to other appropriate department heads or managers.

✔ Be polite, friendly, and specific about your strongest selling points (skills) to perform the job.

For more details and letter samples on self-marketing, consult my book, *Winning Cover Letters,* published by John Wiley & Sons.

## Referral Campaign

In the last year, 63% of all jobs were found through contacts, according to labor studies. "People you know" plus "people you'll get to know" all lead to opening employers' doors and discovering great jobs. Much has been written about networking and using contacts. The referral campaign is a strategy to compile a list of contacts and then expand the list to include people at the companies you've put on your "Employer Prospects" list (p. 104). There's no magic or luck involved in putting together this list.

I remember a software marketing rep who told me, "I don't know anyone."

"Not one single person?" I asked.

"Well, no one in the business . . . no one who can help me."

I smiled and asked, "Oh, so you don't know Bill?"

"Bill?" she questioned.

"Bill Gates, Microsoft's head honcho. Isn't that what you really meant when you said, 'I don't know anyone'?"

I went on to explain that she didn't need to know Bill personally. She really needed to connect with his marketing managers, provided Microsoft was a target, as it was the managers and not Bill who'd hire her.

Start your "Contacts List" (worksheet follows) by listing everyone you *do* know: colleagues, former employees, former bosses, friends, neighbors, family, association executives—anyone you can think of. One client said she got an interview with the president of ABC news because her mother and that president's mother spend their winters together in the same Florida condominium complex and know each other.

Never underestimate where a great connection might come from. A retired 65-year-old mom seemed like an unlikely source for meeting top-notch business contacts—but she was! Remember, everyone knows someone and it may be that new someone who can be of the most help to you.

## CONTACTS LIST

| Name | Title | Company | Phone or E-mail | Referred by | Notes |
|------|-------|---------|-----------------|-------------|-------|
|      |       |         |                 |             |       |
|      |       |         |                 |             |       |
|      |       |         |                 |             |       |
|      |       |         |                 |             |       |
|      |       |         |                 |             |       |
|      |       |         |                 |             |       |
|      |       |         |                 |             |       |

# Networking

Your network of contacts needs to be developed and nurtured during your career. Ed, an aerospace engineer, never bothered with anyone outside of his job. He had no network to speak of. He belonged to no professional or civic organizations. When a major layoff caught his employer by storm, he had a difficult time. He told me, "I guess I really was remiss about developing a network. It didn't seem important. I wish I'd done it, because now I don't know how to start."

I suggested he contact his college's alumni office to see if they had an alumni network in place that might help him. They did. A few alums offered to pass on his resumé, which led him to a terrific new job with Motorola.

Rachel, on the other hand, was the "networking queen." An executive director for a prestigious association, she generously helped everyone who knocked on her door. She also made professional friends as well as contacts. Twice she'd been asked by colleagues to apply for positions she had not even been seeking. Both times she did indeed land the job. The networking she did on an ongoing basis kept her in a visible role—people thought of Rachel when they needed to hire someone with her skills.

**Developing a good network is a career necessity.**

Networking has changed *a lot* over the years. The "good old boys" concept still exists, but now it's both girls *and* boys who are moving ahead. Here are some guidelines to develop a strong network to support your career:

✔ *Help others.*   By becoming a resource to others, you'll ingratiate yourself to others, and they will help you in return.

✔ *Aid those who can never help you.*   You'll have opportunities to provide advice or information to people who are starting out or who are much below your own level. They will unlikely be able to repay you, as they will rarely run into your circle of influence. I have found that the universe rewards our generosity, and although these people may not be able to help you, someone else whom you couldn't repay has probably helped you. It's a life cycle of reaping what you've sown.

✔ *Be visible.*   Let people know who you are, what your expertise is, and that you're a resource they can call on.

✔ *Join organizations.*   Be an active member in a group or groups by attending meetings and volunteering for various tasks that need to be done.

✔ *Seek leadership positions.* Everyone knows the club's president or the conference's coordinator. This is a great way to become and remain known.

✔ *Develop your skills.* Select positions that allow you to develop your skills and move ahead professionally.

✔ *Set goals for making network connections.* Time pressures require us to choose wisely the groups we join and the meetings we attend. Always have a list of five or six key people you'd like to meet, and look for opportunities to introduce yourself and get to know them.

✔ *Be a good conversationalist.* Polish your skills so you are comfortable talking to strangers. Give them your individual attention and interest. Asking questions about them, their goals, or their role in their company is a good conversation opener.

✔ *Be realistic.* Networking is a supportive addition to your arsenal; you gain potential helpers, but they cannot solve all your problems or take on the responsibility to find you a job. Limit the demands you make on any one contact so as not to alienate that person.

✔ *Have a success plan when attending conferences, trade shows, or major meetings.* Decide in advance what you hope to learn. Try to meet two or three people with whom you spend time and could call again in the future. "Working the room" to take home two dozen business cards from people who are clueless as to who you are will be of little or no help later.

✔ *Take the initiative.* Make the effort and approach those people you wish to meet. Call them and ask their advice. Suggest lunch. Make it your responsibility to make the effort.

✔ *Introduce yourself.* It's courteous to introduce (or reintroduce) yourself to others. Be sure to use a memory tag such as "I'm Shannon Bender, a loan officer for Chase Manhattan Bank." Memory tags help people better remember who you are and what you do. If you are unemployed, just say, "Hello, I'm Tom Maxwell, a project manager." If they ask who you work for, mention your former employer, but also state, "I left recently and am currently looking for a new position." Don't be embarrassed or afraid to mention this—they may know of a job.

✔ *Nurture your network.* Develop the relationships by calling, sending notes or e-mails, or passing on articles or resources of interest.

✔ *Thank others.* Always have a supply of thank-you cards, and make the effort to polish off a note and mail it along to anyone who's been helpful to you.

✔ *Recognize and applaud success in others.* Celebrate people's successes. Send a card and short note to congratulate them on promotions, new jobs, or other important achievements.

✔ *Make time for your network.* Return phone calls within 24 hours. Someone with a pressing business problem needs your help now, not in a week or two. You can always limit a call by saying you have a meeting in 10 minutes, but you'll create more friends (and appear more professional) when you return calls promptly.

✔ *Ask for what you need.* Never assume someone won't help you. *Ask*—you'll be amazed how often other people do help. Be specific and clear about your request, no matter what it is. It's better to say, "I'm job hunting, Kathy. Do you know anyone over at 3M in the purchasing department?" versus, "Do you know about any jobs? I need a job."

✔ *Make networking a part of your lifetime career management.* Networking and developing contacts is a lifelong process that aids you throughout your career. Your network can offer guidance and advice to solve problems on the job and can be instrumental in helping you find a new job when the time comes to do that, too.

## Informational Interviews

This is an important tool we covered in Chapter 4, "The Persuasion Package" (see pp. 60–62). This technique—conducting 15-minute interviews to obtain job, organizational, or industry information—is one of the more valuable techniques you can use. By combing your contacts and network you can speak to hiring managers and employers directly. You'll learn firsthand what their needs are and the skills they value to do the job. The following are some general guidelines for conducting informational interviews.

### INFORMATIONAL INTERVIEWING SUCCESS SECRETS

✔ Initial appointments established through referral from another person, introductory letter, or phone call.

✔ Lead-ins or purpose for contact can be varied:
—Would like advice on job search/resumé.
—Discuss vocational interest.
—Desire information on field, industry, or geographical area.

✔ Reassure the person that you don't expect him or her to have a job opening or even know about a job, that you are simply looking for guidance and input to help you better direct your job search.

✔ Be specific about time being requested—usually 15 minutes.

✔ Prepare for the interview. Read company and agency literature. Know what information you plan to request. Write out your questions, which may include:
—Duties of person, major responsibilities, salary ranges.
—Functions or structure of organization.
—Trends in field.
—Procedures, products, programs used or being developed.
—Sources for additional information.
—Suggestions for entry or development into a particular position, field, industry, or company.

✔ Make a positive impression:
—Arrive early for interview.
—Dress well.
—Introduce yourself to receptionist.
—Consider having a business card.
—Have a resumé and references available in case you are asked.

✔ At the start of the meeting, reintroduce yourself and state your reason for being there. Summarize your background and credentials in the first 60 seconds. This will save time and allow you to ask specific questions and get answers in the time allotted.

✔ Ask for referrals to others you could contact, plus suggestions on other companies to approach.

✔ Send a handwritten thank you note.

**INFORMATIONAL INTERVIEW TELEPHONE SCRIPT**

"Good morning, ABC Company."
"[Contact name], please. [Your name] calling."
"Just a moment."
"This is [contact]."

"[Contact], this is [your name], and I was given your name by an acquaintance of yours [referral name]. She told me that you were quite knowledgeable in the field of [your field]. It would be so helpful to me if you could spend 15 minutes answering some questions to assist me in my job search. Let me reassure you, I don't expect you to know about a job, nor do I expect you to have a job. It's really the information and guidance that I'm looking for. Would Monday work or is Tuesday of next week better for you? Morning or afternoon? Great. Thank you, I appreciate your assistance."

**Appointment date:** _____ **Time:** _____

**Location:** _____

_____

_____

**Questions to ask:** _____

_____

_____

Once you've arranged the meeting, be sure you have clear directions on how to get to the meeting site. Next, prepare the questions you wish to ask. You can really inquire about anything you wish to know—you're in the driver's seat. It works best, though, to ask the most important questions first, before you run out of time.

When you arrive at the meeting, be friendly, shake the person's hand, and remind them about the visit's purpose; then quickly summarize your background. Typical questions you might ask could include the following:

✔ What are the most important skills needed to be successful in this job?

✔ What is the most pressing problem or challenge the field faces?

✔ I anticipate the salary range for this job to be between $40,000 and $45,000. Is that about right, or is it too low or too high?

✔ Tell me more about . . .

✔ What are your current growth plans?

✔ Any other questions you want answered.

**TWO IMPORTANT STEPS TO CONDUCT DURING AN INFORMATIONAL INTERVIEW**

- Show the contact your employer prospect list. Ask if he or she knows anyone who works for any of the companies listed. Ask your contact for names of other companies you should consider adding to your prospect list.

- Inquire if there are any other people the contact can think of who would be helpful for you to talk to.

Don't waste people's time. They've been generous enough to try to assist you. Be prepared to make the most of the meeting.

If you are fortunate enough to be meeting at the person's place of employment, you'll benefit from an inside view of what the company's corporate culture is like. Many companies have been removed from a client's prospect list after the job hunter got a brief look inside and did not like what he or she saw.

Upon completion of any informational interview, complete the summary form that follows. Take a few minutes to fill it out while every thing is still fresh in your mind so you don't forget anything.

**INFORMATIONAL INTERVIEW SUMMARY**

| | |
|---|---|
| **Contact:** | |
| **Company:** | **Title:** |
| **Referred by:** | **Date:** |
| **Impression of contact:** | |
| **Impression of company:** | |
| **Key information gained on career goal, company, field:** | |
| **Potential job opportunities mentioned:** | |
| **Evaluation of meeting:** | |
| **Referrals:** | |
| **Next steps:** | |
| **Date thank-you note was sent:** | |

## Hiring Chart

The purpose of the Hiring Chart is to identify the most important skills the employer wants to perform a specific job. During the job hunting process it is used to learn the employer's needs and to correlate those needs with your ability to perform the job. As we discussed in Chapter 4, "The Persuasion Package" (pp. 55–74), the Hiring Chart can also serve as an important tool during salary negotiations.

Introduce the Hiring Chart during an informational interview, and ask for the employer's comments. Have you noted all the important skills needed to do the job? Have you overlooked anything? Have you hit on anything that the employer considers minor? When you are talking to potential bosses, getting these answers provides extremely valuable insight. *Learning how to target your strengths and abilities to meet the employer's needs is the key to getting hired.*

Your Hiring Chart follows. Take a few minutes to break down the major job responsibilities needed to perform the job you want and then list your experience and accomplishments in that area. Refer to the Hiring Chart example in Chapter 4 (p. 64–66) to see the detail and scope this tool should take on.

**Your Name:**

| THE HIRING CHART | |
|---|---|
| **Needs** | **Contributions** |
|  |  |
|  |  |
|  |  |
|  |  |
|  |  |
|  |  |
|  |  |
|  |  |
|  |  |

# Internet

New grads, Generation Xers, high-tech and computer people are all online and viewing the Internet as the newest job source. Indeed, hundreds of thousands of jobs are listed on the Internet. The vast majority are still in the high-tech field. Small companies are unlikely to scan resumés or do electronic searches unless they are in the high-tech arena. Large companies may or may not be actively taking resumés off the information superhighway. A resumé "scanned" by personnel has proved to be a very ineffective job-hunting method. Write directly to the hiring manager (your potential boss) using a targeted letter (or even e-mail). You will get much better results.

For the majority, the Internet has one major value: It is a terrific source of information about jobs, companies, cities, and fields. So far, the Internet has proved itself to be a great research tool. This does not mean that jobs aren't advertised on the Internet. Thousands are added every week. The problems are as follows:

✔ There is no universal index to sort out the jobs you want in the geographical location you wish to be. Just finding the specific jobs that interest you can take an enormous amount of time.

✔ Listings may be months old by the time you find them.

Those in the high-tech fields, those eager (or willing) to relocate, or those with a lot of time on their hands might consider checking out these sites for potential opportunities.

**WEB SITES TO CHECK OUT**

http://www.jobtrak.com/job guide
http://www.jobbankusa.com
http://www.espan.com
http://www.careermosaic.com
http://www.monster.com
http://www.careermag.com
http://www.ajb.dni.us
http://www.careerpath.com
http://www.jobweb.org/
http://www.jobsfed.com/fedjob4.htm
http://www.fjob.mail.opm.gov
http://www.coolworks.com/showme
http://www.occ.com/occ

### Salary Surveys

http://www.jobsmart.org/jobsmart

Many clients report that they've found extensive employer information and critical salary surveys on the Internet. These are both valid reasons to utilize this technique in your search process.

*Caution: Extensive Time to Find the Openings.* This remains the biggest drawback concerning the Internet. Yet the Internet has changed its face in the five seconds it took me to write this sentence. I've included the Internet because it has the potential to be a significant source of job leads as more and more of America gets online. Depending on your field, your willingness to relocate, and the type of job you seek, it may prove to be worth the effort spent to locate employers and jobs.

## You Can Do It

You can and will get a new position if you control your destiny. Don't wait for an employer to make it happen. Try new techniques, set goals, do the extra work. The hidden job market is extra work—hard work with no immediate payoff. But consider the odds—85% of all jobs are here, and the crowd is *not*. It's just you and a few others.

My clients and seminar participants mail in hundreds of testimonials each year confirming that these techniques have worked well and aided them in landing terrific jobs. If you use these techniques, your job search will yield better openings with better companies. You can control your success and outcome, but extra work is the price. Is it worth it? You bet it is! The facts tell us that most of the new jobs lie with small employers. Networking and referrals are the best way to hear about them. The Hiring Chart allows you to learn directly from potential bosses what skills they value. Market research identifies companies that match your interests. Targeted letters knock on the doors you want to enter. All this adds up to taking a proactive stance: controlling your future to find the most rewarding job possible and make it yours.

### PAVING THE WAY

These techniques are the roadway to the main event: the interview. It's during the interview that you either land the job or lose it. Those 24 hours of preparation must be used to maximize your competitive edge. Use your contacts and research skills to pull together as much information as possible to prepare for your job interview. You've gotten the employer's interest with all the job hunting techniques you've used so far. Now, you must know what to say and how to truly market the best you have to offer. On to the main event—your interview.

# EXCEL IN THE INTERVIEW

## YOU

*You are nature's greatest miracle. All men are your brothers, yet you are different from each. Do not imitate others. Put your uniqueness on display, you are rare, and there is value in all rarity.*

*Be a master of your emotions. Try to sing when you feel depressed and laugh when you feel sad. Try each day to bring joy, enthusiasm, and laughter into the lives of others, and automatically joy, enthusiasm, and laughter will become a part of yours. Remove from your vocabulary negative words such as* quit, cannot, impossible, *and* hopeless, *for they are words of the nondoers.*

*Waste not a moment of your life mourning yesterday's mistakes, defeats, or heartaches, for that would be throwing good after bad. Life is a measure of time; do not waste time, or you will waste life. Destroy procrastination with action, destroy doubt with faith, and destroy fear with confidence. Act now: the procrastination which has held you back is no longer a part of your life.*

*Though you may stumble and fall, realize that few march straight to success and happiness. Persist until you succeed, knowing this is one of the greatest principles of success.*

*—ANONYMOUS*

Nothing could be worse than this," stated Carol, a panic-filled 39-year-old utility division manager. "I have to interview for my own job. This merger [between the gas company and Carol's power company] is turning out to be an employee's nightmare. I've been here for 11 years—now I could lose my job! Help me," she continued, desperation and anxiety emphasizing every word. "I've got to do well in the interview." Carol was scared—rightfully so. Her company was living through a merger that had rocked the entire power industry. As more and more gas and power companies joined forces, thousands of employees lost their jobs. As a manager, Carol was very vulnerable. She was terrified about her upcoming interview; although she tried to bolster herself, she realized everything was on the line.

Carol was not certain *how* to begin. She hadn't interviewed for a job in 10 years. "I don't have a degree," she said. "That'll hurt me, won't it?" Carol needed reassurance, and, more important, she needed a game plan to approach the upcoming interview. Every job interview is critical: If you blow it, you won't get the job. A great deal is at stake. Carol realized this, and you should, too.

Carol was relieved to learn that certain persuasion tools would help ease the process. We developed her 5 Point Agenda (Chapter 4, pp. 59–60) and her 60 Second Sell (Chapter 4, pp. 57–59). We worked on her answers for many of the typical questions she'll likely be asked.

I advised her to put together some examples of her work. She had received some good evaluations on the various projects she managed; copies would be made to bring along and give to the interviewer. Carol was worried about not having a degree. A great deal of her fear arose from that fact, suspecting it might be the reason she'd lose her job. "I should have gone to college," Carol told me. "But with working and raising my daughter there never seemed time. It didn't matter much then, unfortunately. I see how important a college degree would be now." I asked Carol if she'd ever taken any company-sponsored courses. "A ton," she said. "I'm involved with commercial installation, and I have an extensive background in gas and power coordination, distribution, networks, and transmissions. I've had a great deal of training here in the utility technology, engineering, and project management also."

"In your specific industry and job, Carol," I replied, "all that coursework is tremendously valuable. It is not something anyone obtains at college, since it's job and industry specific. You can make a strong case that although you may lack a formal degree, you have more than made up for it with all the courses you've taken from your gas company. Could you make a list of all the courses you've taken to give to the interviewer?"

"Yes, I never even thought about all the company training, but as you point out, I could make a case for how it was more relevant to my job," Carol replied.

"Add that to your evaluations," I stated. "And you have a strong candidacy for the job."

Carol's other worry came when she learned that the interview would be with a panel of four people: two from HR (one from her company, the other from the power company) and two managers she did not know. I suggested she treat this interview as though she weren't an insider. No one would be familiar with her or her work, so she must approach it as she would a new employer to make a strong case for her candidacy. I also gave her some advice on handling the situation. "A panel interview is one of the most stressful interviewing situations there is. As each person asks a question, topics jump from one to another, making it difficult to establish a rhythm and rapport. To get off to a good start, smile and shake the hand of each interviewer. Repeat each one's name: "Nice to meet you, Bob," "Hello, Mary," and so on. A firm handshake and a warm smile relaxes everyone and "warms them up" to be more receptive to you as a candidate. During the interview, maintain solid eye contact with the person who asks the question. Don't look away to the others, or the person asking the question will be left with the impression that you don't care about his or her concerns. And, of course, a nice conservative suit is mandatory, so you'll appear professional to everyone.

Carol used the 24 hours before the interview well. She had compiled her "proof"—performance evaluations, a list of training courses she'd taken, project spreadsheets, and budget reallocations she'd implemented. She had insightful questions to ask, had written out succinct answers to questions she might be asked, and had her lucky penny in her purse. She was ready.

At two o'clock she went to the interview. She was very nervous, but found that smiling helped. The introductions went fine. The panel members started out with some explanations of the new jobs and the objectives. Carol was ready for their first question.

PANEL: Tell us about your background and what you would bring to this job.

CAROL: [*The 60 Second Sell provided an appropriate answer.*] For the last five years I've managed projects and teams involved in commercial gas installation. I've had extensive in-house training in engineering, regulations, distribution, networks, transmission, and safety. I've excelled at resource management, adapting to change, and have been good at maximizing shrinking budgets. Two key strengths I'd bring to the job are project management and people skills. Utilizing computerized systems and timeline tracking, I've handled multiple complex projects, coordinating numerous aspects to deliver customer service and produce results on time and within budget. The merger has had a significant morale impact but I've dealt with change as a good and needed element. I've provided information, helped employees redefine their jobs, and notably increased my team's productivity. Finally, I actively adapt and implement the new utility technologies, such as real time, AMR, and wireless—our future depends on quickly learning and using these technologies in our jobs. That's a significant part of what makes the job interesting and enjoyable to me. I think that sums up in a nutshell what I'd bring to the job and new company.

PANEL: [*Several technical questions were asked, all of which Carol answered knowledgeably. Then they began to quantify her "management" ability.*] Tell us about your experience adapting resources and budgets to the 10% decrease implemented last year.

CAROL: Certainly. In fact, I brought a project spreadsheet I did at the time to show you exactly how I approached the problem. [*She passed out copies of the spreadsheet to each member of the panel.*] I prepared a computerized analysis of all costs and functions. By redefining some tasks and reassigning job duties, I was able to lower people costs by combining jobs for better staff utilization. We trimmed down warehoused materials and did more just-in-time planning. This allowed us to cut 11% from our budget by year-end.

PANEL: Working with unions can result in handling some difficult situations. Explain a specific incident in which you dealt with a difficult worker on a productivity/performance issue.

CAROL: [*She had thought they'd ask this and had prepared an answer.*] Let's see . . . Tim's been with the company 23 years. He's a union man, never doing one second more than is absolutely necessary. You can check with HR and notice his record showed marginal performance that was just accepted in the past. Tim had a big problem "taking orders from any woman," I'd been told. When he first came to my team, I gave him a chance to prove himself. When he did not work up to my other team members' standards, I sat him down and told him so. I also knew saving face was very important to Tim. While I laid out areas he needed to quickly improve in, I pointed out some strengths and praised him for those. I told him once he got up to speed in the other areas, I planned to have him lead training on regulations since he was well versed in that area. We agreed on a performance plan and met weekly. Tim showed significant improvement over the next few months and is now a more valued team member.

PANEL: What is your philosophy and approach with customers?

CAROL: My entire career has involved customer service. I know a large part of my job is education—to clearly make customers aware of timelines, deal with outages quickly, resolve problems, and explain technology and product information. With deregulation, we've had to be better at meeting and satisfying our customers' needs. We no longer have the monopoly we used to have before deregulation. Now, our competitors are eager to steal our customers. I've tried to be available to customers, with clear and open lines of communication. I have everyone on the team functioning in the problem-solving mode. There are times when utility technology is not as advanced as clients want, so I always try to present options and alternatives. I guess my approach is summed up by saying I try to create a long-term, happy partnership with customers.

PANEL: Downsizing has been stressful on everyone. How are you dealing with it?

CAROL: No one likes having their job threatened. I don't; most employees don't. I acknowledge that everyone—me included—is intimidated by the situation. I also point out that change is necessary for us to survive in the industry. I started a brown-bag lunch group where people could freely and openly express their concerns. I have had HR in to talk to the group. Ken, our top department head, and a couple trainers also spoke on handling change. Nothing eliminates the fear, but the open communication helps. I've had an open-door policy and squelched some incredible rumors—paranoia got pretty widespread there for a while. On a personal note, I exercise three or four times a week after work, and I found that to be helpful in alleviating the pressure, stress, and emotional demands all the downsizing has produced.

PANEL: What do you see as the major problems facing the company and your division in the future?

CAROL: Improving productivity, motivating old workers to change into what we need to go forward. Implementing more AMR and real-time computer-based wireless data transmission. I've taken a lot of courses in these new technologies recently, but our competitors are ahead in terms of utilizing these technologies. So we need to move forward quickly to stay competitive in our industry's changing marketplace.

Carol was then given time to ask questions. Most dealt with technical and organizational issues and then a couple on the interview process and what she could expect. Two weeks later, she heard she got the job. One of the interviewers called her and shared this insight with her. "Carol," he confided, "prior to the interview, employees were ranked. You had no degree, and since this job required a strong engineering/technical background, you came up short. But you really did well in the interview. The spreadsheet, the company training you had, those letters from customers, and feedback from your boss moved you way up the ladder. I'm pleased to tell you the entire committee agreed you are an asset as a division manager and that we want you to keep working for us. You got the job."

Preparation is essential for any job interview. The first step is to analyze your strengths. The 5 Point Agenda (see Chapter 4) is the best tool to do this. Carol identified her top five selling points to reiterate throughout the interview:

1. Technical/utility experience

2. Resource management

3. Project management

4. People/team development skills

5. New technology skills

Armed with her 5 Point Agenda and 60 Second Sell, she wrote out questions and was able to relax once the interview started. She felt she had good answers to the questions. Her confidence was an important underscore to convince the panel to select her for the job. Carol told me, "I really learned a lot through this process. I don't feel powerless anymore. I discovered my value and learned to emphasize my strengths. I even learned how to counter my weaknesses. The lack of a degree didn't stop me from getting the job. But if I hadn't used your persuasion tools and followed your advice and game plan, I would have lost the job. I actually survived this whole process. I heard that several dozen other division managers got laid off. The whole experience is something I hope I never go through again, but I'm grateful I realized exactly what I could offer the company *before* the interview."

**CAREER COACH** *tip*

**Preparation is the key to interview success.**

# *5 Point Agenda*

The foundation of the interview is your 5 Point Agenda. This persuasion tool (see Chapter 4) analyzes the job you are about to interview for. It reviews your own knowledge about performing the job, plus any additional information you glean from company research or contacts. Be sure to call everyone you know who might know a person inside the prospective company who could offer additional insight.

One client, Daniel, told me how developing a 5 Point Agenda helped him:

> I got ecstatic when my dream organization called me for an interview. The job was to be a program coordinator at a college. I was thrilled I'd made it this far. I quickly went to work and created my 5 Point Agenda based on a complete job description I'd had personnel fax to me. I looked over my contacts and knew a colleague who had once worked for the college. I called her, and she passed on a contact in the department where I planned to interview. She even called that man— José—to pave the way for my call. That conversation happened the day before my interview. José gave me tremendous insight into the job. Although marketing programs was one of my strengths, I had not even included it as one of my five points. He told me marketing was the only thing the department cared about. In the next 24 hours, I redid my 5 Point Agenda, created a 60 Second Sell, pulled together some work examples, and prepped my answers to possible questions. The interview was two hours with a panel of six. Competition was steep: 500 resumés and eight people interviewed. But I got the job! I later learned I beat out the inside candidate everyone thought was a shoo-in for the position. My marketing and promotions background— once I emphasized them—really swayed the committee. I credit this tool and the job analysis you recommend in aiding in my success.

## CREATE YOUR 5 POINT AGENDA

**Before the job interview, analyze the job the employer wants you to do and select your top five selling points. Weave these points with specific examples throughout the interview.**

1. _____

_____

**2.** _____

_____

**3.** _____

_____

**4.** _____

_____

**5.** _____

_____

## 60 Second Sell

Over my professional career, this is the one technique that most clients and seminar participants single out as the most helpful tool they've learned in the job search process. Josephine wrote, "I've always found the interview to be particularly difficult. I'm terrific in my position, but I do a very poor job at selling myself. I never knew how to approach the interview before. I assumed you just showed up. The 60 Second Sell was like a lightbulb turning on for me—a strategy I put to work just 10 days after your seminar. It worked. I just landed a terrific job with one of the country's premier companies."

The 60 Second Sell (reviewed in Chapter 4) is the best way to excel in the interview since it condenses your five selling points into a few sentences. This tool is a powerful way to start an interview—the answer to "Tell me about yourself." The 60 Second Sell is also a strong way to summarize and end an interview, leaving the employer with a lasting impression of your strongest points on how you can perform the job. Whenever the employer asks, "What are your strengths?," "Why should I hire you?," or "What are your proudest accomplishments?," the answer is your 60 Second Sell.

Before your next interview, create your 5 Point Agenda. Weave these five points together into a couple of sentences to create your 60 Second Sell. Now you'll have a powerful tool to use when you sit in front of a potential employer.

**CREATE YOUR 60 SECOND SELL**
Analyze the job.

Select your top five selling points. Link them together in a few sentences to develop your 60 Second Sell. Memorize this statement.

_____
_____
_____
_____
_____
_____
_____

   Both the 5 Point Agenda and the 60 Second Sell should be *newly* created for every interview. Customize them to meet the employer's *specific* needs to perform the job.

# Controlling the Interview

Jim got a call to come in for an interview. As a manufacturing manager at a Fortune 500 company, he'd been laid off a few months before. A friend had helped him get this initial interview. He met with Marilyn, a human resources representative for a toy manufacturer. It was her task to screen potential managers and identify any top candidates to meet with the department supervisor. The position they were trying to fill was engineering supervisor.

   Jim walked in and sat down. He did not offer to shake hands and appeared chatty and nervous, Marilyn noted. She introduced herself.

MARILYN: Tell me about yourself.

JIM: Let's see. I was born in Dayton, Ohio. I enjoy the Midwest. Spent my youth there. I went to Ohio State and got my engineering degree in '74. I spent a couple years at Procter & Gamble and then went to City University and worked on my MBA. Since I was studying and working hard on the degree, I stayed in the design and process area as a tech. Took four years, but I finished and the company offered me a job in New Jersey. But my wife didn't want to move, so I turned it down. That wasn't too smart 'cause they laid me off after that. I found a job with Avon in the product manufacturing division. . . . [*Jim continued on with his history for about 10 more minutes and ended with his last job at Kimberly-Clark in the product manufacturing area.*]

Marilyn's mind started to wander after the first two minutes. She nodded, but no longer concentrated on what Jim was saying. When he finished, she looked at her sheet. After a couple straightforward questions, she added a tricky one, knowing many people had a problem answering this one.

MARILYN: Please identify for me your weakness on the job.

JIM: [*Hesitant, he knew that if she called his old boss he'd say Jim had communications problems with other staff. That's what popped into his head.*] My old boss felt I had a little communication problem with some of the secretaries and nontechnical staff. I'm efficient and like things done correctly. The old company let people get away with shabby work and mistakes, but the new improvement campaign pressured us to improve productivity and get it right the first time. I lose patience with secretaries who don't get it done on time and correctly. My boss seemed to be a little too easy on them—I demanded more and was quick to complain about those who weren't up to snuff. Didn't seem to do much good, which probably explains the company's problems and need for layoffs.

Marilyn did not like the superiority and arrogance in Jim's reply. She thought, "He'll be a problem here with that attitude. Engineers often can't get along, and we need managers with good people skills he lacks. No, he won't work. Plus, notice how he runs down the company and boss—he's a blamer, not a problem solver. He's a *no*." Marilyn made a final notation on his interview evaluation that ended all Jim's possibilities with that company.

Dealing with those tricky questions effectively will influence the interviewer in either a positive or negative way. Taking the time to write out answers to questions you'll likely be asked is a necessary component to add to your persuasion package. Marilyn's question, "What's your greatest weakness?," is a frequently asked inquiry. I teach employers in my hiring seminars to *always* ask this question. The reason? Job hunters usually offer a key piece of information that illustrates they can't perform or are not right for the job. The best way to approach this "weakness" question is to identify a moot point. You could define an old weakness and how you learned to overcome it. For Jim, discussing a weakness unrelated to performing the job well would have been a better way to handle it. A more appropriate answer might have been this:

> In a past evaluation, I was marked lower on my communication skills. I had little patience with mistakes and was viewed as "demanding and critical" by the secretaries. I asked my boss and our HR manager for ways I might improve. I took a few courses and developed a mentor relationship with a manager who excelled in dealing with staff. The next time I was evaluated, I'd showed a noticeable improvement—achieving an above-average rating.

Of course Jim could say this only if it were true. Showing that you are interested in personal improvement and seek to solve problems or deficiencies will be viewed in a positive light. Another possible response if he could not show correction of a former weakness would have been pointing out a nonnecessary skill that he lacked. For example, "Occasionally, I deal with the sales rep in our planning process committee. The sales manager has really got some top-notch selling and presentation skills. I do well leading small groups, but he's amazing in front of the whole division—that's 1,700 people. I get so nervous, if I ever was required to do those division presentations—I'd need more training first.

Notice here Jim points out a skill—large group presentations—something he does not need to possess to do the potential employer's job well. He is careful to state that he's good at small group facilitation (a needed skill) and also indicates that he'd need more training if he were to be responsible for division large group presentations. This shows his adaptability and willingness to learn and take on new responsibilities. Jim needed to develop appropriate answers before the interview to avoid the kind of damage that his answer to the HR rep created. By preparing in advance you can control the interview, because your answers direct the conversation's path. Solid answers and citing previous work and performance examples will be the most influential. Knowing an acceptable answer to tricky questions like the one about your weakness prevents you from making the critical mistakes Jim did.

The following chart contains dozens of questions employers commonly ask. Practice and review these before your next interview.

## QUESTIONS EMPLOYERS OFTEN ASK

✔ Tell me about yourself.

✔ What are your long-range and short-range goals and objectives? How are you preparing yourself to achieve them?

✔ What do you like to do in your spare time?

✔ How would you describe your personality? How would others?

✔ What do you consider to be your greatest strength?

✔ What do you consider to be your greatest weakness?

✔ Why should I hire you?

✔ Describe your ideal supervisor.

✔ Describe yourself as a supervisor.

✔ Describe your worst supervisor.

✔ What was the last book you read?

✔ Why haven't you obtained a job so far?

✔ Describe how you work under pressure, deadlines, etc.

✔ What do you know about our company?

✔ What two or three things are most important to you in your job?

✔ Why did you change jobs so frequently?

✔ Are you willing to travel?

✔ What do you think of our little operation here?

✔ How do you handle pressure and stress?

✔ Why do you want to leave your present job?

✔ Why did you have to leave your last job?

✔ Do you think you can get along with . . . ?

✔ What kind of salary are you looking for?

✔ I'm a little worried about your lack of . . .

✔ We work a lot of late nights here. Is that going to cause any problems?

✔ Do you have commitments that would interfere with your job?

✔ Have you hired or fired many people?

✔ You've had quite a few jobs in your career. Why?

✔ You have too much experience for this job. Why would you want it?

✔ How will you cope with a new organization after so many years at your old company?

✔ What was it about your last job that bothered you the most?

✔ What was it you liked best about your last job?

✔ What motivates you?

✔ How creative a problem solver are you?

✔ How long do you expect to work for us if we offer you the job?

✔ Are you willing to go where the company sends you?

✔ What contributions can we expect if we hire you? How long will it take you to make them?

✔ Do you prefer working with others or by yourself?

✔ What qualities should a successful manager possess?

✔ Describe a large mistake you made at your last job.

✔ What two accomplishments have given you the most satisfaction? Why?

✔ Describe your ideal job.

✔ How do you think your present/last boss would describe you?

✔ Can you motivate people? Give us examples.

✔ If you could be in your own business, would you prefer it to corporate life?

✔ How long do you think you'd be happy in this job before you started thinking about promotion?

✔ What's the most difficult challenge you've faced in your life?

✔ What are you doing now to improve yourself?

✔ Tell me about a time that you dealt with a difficult customer.

✔ What area of your work does your current local boss criticize the most?

✔ Describe a specific conflict (or conflicts) you had with a coworker.

✔ Describe a major problem you've had at work.

✔ Give us examples of the types of computer work you typically do.

Take the time to ponder and work on answers to potential questions. This will allow you to be succinct and persuasive. Our goal is to develop a rapport. Jim's 10-minute introductory answer bored the interviewer, and she stopped listening by the second minute. *A good rule of thumb is to answer a question in less than 60 seconds.*

For more help on answering potential questions, see my book, *60 Seconds & You're Hired!,* in which I offer answers to 80 tough, tricky questions along with an in-depth overview of the entire interview process.

Now let's go back into Marilyn's (our HR manager's) office and see how another candidate did. Marilyn had another interviewee for the same job that Jim didn't get—engineering supervisor. Jim was long since forgotten when the next applicant, Beverly, came in to interview. The bulk of the interview went okay. Marilyn offered Beverly an opportunity to really impress her.

MARILYN: [*Marilyn thought over Beverly's answers. Standard, she thought. I would have liked to have seen more enthusiasm, but technical people are usually less expressive. Okay, let's give her a chance to see what her concerns on the job really are.*] Do you have any questions you'd like to ask, Beverly?

BEVERLY: Yes. What's the salary and benefits package this job offers?

MARILYN: What do you expect?

BEVERLY: I was making $57,000 plus bonus and had full medical, dental, and retirement.

MARILYN: The department supervisor determines the salary and can discuss that with you if you proceed to the second stage of our hiring process.

The interview ended.

Marilyn reviewed Beverly's credentials after she left. She shook her head. "She isn't going to work," Marilyn thought, "Just after a paycheck. No one cares about doing the job anymore. It gets harder and harder to find those special people who really want to work and do well. She'll spend a long time looking in today's market if she doesn't show more interest in the job. Well, she won't get hired here." Marilyn concluded and wrote a "no" on the top of Beverly's resumé.

Beverly's mistake came at a time when she could have really impressed the interviewer. Marilyn gave her the opening when she concluded with, "Do you have any questions?" You see how Beverly missed the boat entirely by asking her question on salary and benefits. Beverly may have wanted to know the answer, but she impressed no one with the question. In Chapter 8, I cover salary issues at length, and one of our first rules of success is never to mention money before the employer does.

Marilyn viewed Beverly's question in a negative light. Don't make that mistake. Create a list of questions that will provide you with insight and information that are key to determining whether the job is a good fit for *you*. Is it a good fit? Will you be able to use skills you enjoy? What are the people like? The company? The politics? What are the advancement opportunities? What are budget priorities and future plans? How will they affect your job in the months ahead? Which software do they use? Which committees will you be involved in? Inquire about potential problems you'll face or any employee conflicts you may need to deal with.

**Use the interview to ask questions and determine whether or not it would be a good job for you.**

Employers want to hire people who show interest in the job and appear sharp and on the ball. Your questions give them the indication of what you do and don't think about. Always bring a list of typed-out questions to ask. When it's your turn, bring out the list and go over the questions. You can use the phrase, "Let's see, we covered my questions on your computer systems and process procedures." This indicates that these were concerns of yours, but you don't have to rehash something that was covered. Mentioning it will suffice.

Michael, a top executive at a Fortune 100 company told me, "The most important part of the interview is the time the candidate asks his or her questions. I get some insight into how they think and their level of interest in being a contributor to my company." Many other employers I've spoken with have agreed with this statement.

Don't miss this important opportunity to impress the employer and show you are the right person for the job. And most important, this may be your only opportunity to gather facts and information to determine if this would be a happy and good fit for you.

Now let's visit Tim, a human resources manager about to interview Matt for a position in his company. Matt graduated from college six months ago. A friend's mom helped arrange this interview at MCI.

TIM: So, Matt, tell me, what have you done since graduation?

MATT: I went to Europe as a graduation present. It was really cool. I got back in September and began to look for a job.

TIM: [*He noticed that Matt was very nervous.*] What positions are you interested in?

MATT: Well—management. I got my B.S. in business.

TIM: What area?

**A clear job target is essential to focus and sell your skills to an employer.**

MATT: [*Confidently.*] I want to be in management. I'm great leading a team. I was captain of our college soccer team. I am good at getting everyone motivated and I'm a leader.

Tim thought to himself, "Typical new grad. Has no idea what he wants to do and thinks you can start at the top. He hasn't a clue as to what 'management' is. He's only worked at McDonald's and on construction jobs. Well, I haven't got time to figure out if he could do anything here." Shortly thereafter, Tim ended the interview.

A huge mistake many job hunters make, especially new grads, is to not have a clear focus about what they want to do. Job hunters need to offer specific job titles and areas, which Matt didn't do. He should have read through the company's literature and asked his friends for more inside information on specific job duties.

Matt needed to do some career exploration in order to make some decisions and become more knowledgeable about specific job functions. Let's return to our HR manager Tim's office as he now prepares to interview another recent grad, Andrea.

TIM: So, what have you done in the last six months since college?

ANDREA: I spent time job hunting while I worked at the Gap. I wanted to use my communications degree, but it seemed no one wanted to hire me without experience. Four months ago, I began to volunteer two mornings a week at the Lung Association. I've worked on the flyers and fundraising materials. Here are some samples I've done. [*She hands them to Tim.*] Plus they now have me help with their newsletter—here's an article I worked on. [*She also gives this to him.*]

TIM: These are quite impressive. I'm curious—why volunteer?

ANDREA: How else would I get experience when no one would give me a chance? I'm a quick learner and excellent on the computer. And the Lung Association is a good cause to donate my time to.

TIM: So, what kind of position are you looking for?

ANDREA: I've watched your job listings. I'd like to be in the communications area, but marketing is interesting, too. I'm a good writer and can create flyers, brochures, and complex documents on my PC. I'm great at research and have learned a lot about program marketing and mailing lists at the Lung Association.

TIM: Why should I hire you?

ANDREA: [*She used her 60 Second Sell.*] I have a solid education and foundation in the communications area. I'm a great writer and terrific on the computer conducting research or creating newsletters and flyers. I'm a fast learner and put in a lot of extra time in my off hours to learn the best ways to do something. I'm very productive and use my time well. I think if you check with my boss at the Lung Association you'll find I've contributed a great deal since I've been there.

Tim thought, "She's got initiative and shows a great deal of potential. I'll call her boss and then send her on to Jason in corporate relations and see what he thinks." He notes that she's to be given a second interview.

When Andrea returned the following week to meet with Jason, she landed a job.

Andrea had a good idea of what she wanted to do. When she lacked experience, she volunteered to get some. This impressed the interviewer. The HR manager also saw high standards and quality in the work she showed him. She was focused and had good answers and examples to support the assumption she'd work out well. Andrea was focused in a way Matt, who wanted to be in management, was not. This made it easier for her to identify the skills the employer would want and market them appropriately.

## *The Interview Success Formula*

Utilizing the 24 hours before the job interview will result in doing your very best to positively influence an employer. Implement the following 21 guidelines to maximize your effectiveness and preparation efforts.

1. *Analyze the job and company.* Call any contact you have to get an insiders' perspective on the job. Go to the library or use the Internet to download information and recent articles about the company. At the very least, learn what they do; know the company's products or services sold.

2. *Get a job description.* Personnel or the person calling to arrange the interview may be able to fax you a complete, up-to-date job description. Ask questions. Try to learn as much as possible from that person about the needs of the job.

3. *Create your 5 Point Agenda.* This is customized to define your five top selling points for the job in question.

4. *Create your 60 Second Sell.* This will be the perfect answer to "Tell me about yourself," "What are your strengths?," Why should I hire you?" It's also the best way to summarize and end an interview. The 60 Second Sell links together your top five selling points in a few sentences you can say in 60 seconds.

5. *Bring evidence of your work.* Bring copies of work—examples—that the employer can see. Displaying a spreadsheet of a project outline is much more influential than just "telling" about it. Select some tangible evidence that will testify to your stated abilities and performance.

6. *Write out answers to potential questions.* Clearly think through how to best answer potential questions. Write up and review answers to be succinct. Offer specifics of what you've done in the past. Be sure to have answers for hard questions: "Why do want to leave your job?" "What's your weakness?" These answers will be much easier to develop when you are not on the hot seat to provide them.

7. *Answer questions in less than 60 seconds.* One-word answers are too short, but lengthy, babbling replies lose the interviewer's interest. Be succinct and clear, offering details in a concise way.

8. *Offer plenty of examples.* Employers hire based on their estimation that what you've done in the past is likely how you'll perform for them in the future. Use examples that paint pictures. Instead of saying, "I'm a good organizer," describe the special event or project you planned and the success it achieved.

9. *Offer only solid references.* Not everyone will sing our praises. Prepare a list of work references who have either supervised you or dealt with you extensively and can give a firsthand report on your work and performance. In most cases, employers call those three people you've identified. Hand an interviewer a typed list that has verified and accurate phone numbers. Always be certain that a reference offers only positive information. Eliminate anyone you believe may give any negative information—it's better to replace a reference than lose the job because someone said something uncomplimentary about you.

10. *Create a list of questions to ask.* Type a list of questions that will help you determine if the company and job are an ideal, or at least a good fit for you. Ask only job- and organization-related questions. Any salary or benefits questions need to wait until the job offer has been made.

11. *Practice your delivery.* Use a tape recorder to hear how you sound. Ask a friend to role play and interview you, or visit a career counselor for professional help to work on your verbal responses and nonverbal delivery.

12. *Dress professionally.* Select an outfit, planner/organizer, and other materials that announce you are indeed an asset to any company you work for.

13. *Smile.* Emphasize your confidence and professionalism by smiling often, but only when appropriate. Employers want friendly, nice people to work with.

14. *Use a firm handshake.* Be sure to work on this. Smile, grip firmly, look into the person's eyes, and say their name.

15. *Maintain eye contact.* Always focus on the person asking the question to maintain his or her attention and involvement in what you are saying.

16. *Listen carefully and answer the questions asked.* If you are unclear on anything, ask the employer for clarification before you answer.

17. *Create a conversation.* Build rapport by asking some questions as you go. If they bring up computer skills, inquire about the systems and applications they use. Then respond by addressing their needs with any related experience you have to offer.

18. *Show respect.* Employers make their own judgments. Always remain positive. Do not share negative comments about old bosses and companies. Don't use "puff" statements (e.g., "You'll never get anyone as good as me") in closing. The 60 Second Sell is more effective and allows them solid evidence to justify their decisions on your potential and strengths.

19. *Demonstrate interest and enthusiasm.* Monotones and a poker face won't convince the employer you are a strong contender. Use vocal variety and enthusiasm in your voice. Radiate interest and

energy about doing the job, confidently offering past-performance examples to show how you'll succeed in this position.

20. *Send a thank-you note.*   Many a job was clinched when a simple but persuasive thank-you note was received within 48 hours after the interview. Personalize the comments by handwriting or typing them in a positive, enthusiastic tone. Define three or four points that demonstrate why you would succeed at this job. Always thank the interviewer for the opportunity, even if it's a job you no longer want. That courtesy may be remembered for a better job down the line.

21. *Program your mind for success.*   Review your strengths. Listen to motivational tapes. Have a friend give you a pep talk. Repeat only positive affirmations in your mind. "I will succeed." "I'm a good worker." "They will quickly see my value for their company." Stay positive and avoid any and all negative influences before your interview.

## Dealing with Failure

All of us face times when our best is not what the employer needs or wants. Sometimes the competition is so tight that, although they agree you'd do a fine job, so would a couple of the other candidates, one of whom gets the job. There are ways to handle the news that you were not selected that can often result in being hired later on.

Many disappointed candidates, when not selected, call and ask the employer "why." They expect an honest answer, but instead get a pat reply that "the other person's experience was more of what we wanted." It's a rare employer who'll truthfully tell you why you failed. Too many worry about litigation. Even if they wanted to help, they are often afraid to. You will get further if you handle the rejection the way I recommend my clients do. For example, Candice called to inquire whether the employer with whom she'd interviewed had made a selection. The interviewer told her the job went to someone else. Here's how she responded:

> Well I'm sorry that it didn't work out, Theresa [the interviewer's name]. I liked your company and felt that my background in product development would be an asset. Let me reaffirm that I'm still interested in the job. If the person selected does not work out, please reconsider me for the position. If another job comes up that is applicable, please keep me in mind. Any chance you might be aware of another company who might need my skills?

With this follow-up, Candice planted the seeds, plus asked for a referral. This approach has led many clients to learn about other potential jobs. Two months after the interview, Candice did get the job when the first person they hired did not work out.

I've had numerous clients who told me companies called a month or two later when a different job became available. They'd been remembered, and the new job was deemed a better fit with the client's abilities. Professionally handling a rejection by leaving an open door is a strategy few job hunters practice, but one that can be quite effective and produce success. Always end on a strong, positive note.

## Beware of Pity Parties

Disappointment is natural when you hope to land an important job. In this book and in all my other books, I try to offer the best advice possible to eliminate most mistakes people make that can cause them to fail. Still, there will be setbacks. Everyone has them. But how you react makes a big difference to your long-term success. Pity parties—feeling sorry for yourself—that last weeks or months at a time destroy your future. Therefore, always have a game plan and options laid out. If you missed out on the job, you can have a one-day pity party. Feel sorry for yourself. Have a woe-is-me day where you really sulk. Then get over it! Exercise. Call your friends for support. Read my books to implement new strategies. Take some positive action. Consult a career counselor. But remember, a setback is only a temporary disappointment. A newspaper reporter once asked Babe Ruth about his large number of strike-outs. His reply was, "I'm always swinging for the fence. Sometimes I make it and sometimes I don't, but I always go after the goal, no matter how often I fail." You must push forward even when you're discouraged. In the very near future, you'll be the happy one who gets the job, and others will be having pity parties because they didn't. So don't let a setback (and that's all this is) derail you. Many clients found the very next job and interview was a better fit, and that was the job they went on to land.

**CAREER COACH** *tip*

**Failure is never fatal unless you lose the courage to try again.**
—*ROBIN RYAN*

# GET PROMOTED!

## ACHIEVEMENT

*Winston Churchill gave the commencement address at his prep school, Harrow, where his own academic performance was less than outstanding.*

*Churchill, one of the world's greatest orators, walked up to the podium, looked over the crowd, and said, "Never give up." He paused again and said, "Never give up." He paused again and said, "Never, ever, give up." That said, he sat down.*

Jonathan, a research scientist at a large pharmaceutical company, believes he has found a formula to prevent cancer. This breakthrough will be as important as the polio vaccine. He thinks of the Nobel Prize he'll surely win when he proves his discovery. Surely this will make him a division head at the company. He must inform his superiors to obtain the funding to conduct all necessary experiments and trials to bring his idea to fruition. The former lab director, also a scientist, lost his job during a recent downsizing and reorganization. This leaves the research scientist no option but to go to the company VP. He enters the meeting well prepared—with slides and graphs of molecules. He begins to tell the VP of his discovery and offers all the scientific data he's amassed to support his hypothesis. The VP is quickly lost—molecules, enzymes—he has no idea what the scientist is saying or what he wants. At the end he asks, "What exactly do you want and what does it cost?" The figure of $2 to $3 million was all the VP heard. "No. Absolutely not—we haven't the budget and, besides, it won't work." (*Anything costing that much is out of the question, what with our budget crunch,* the VP thinks.) The scientist, completely dejected, leaves, never realizing he was turned down because the VP had no idea *what* he was talking about.

You won't excel without developing *persuasion skills.* Your career is becoming more dependent on your ability to communicate, persuade, influence, and take initiative.

I've discovered that three major factors influence career direction as people seek to obtain promotions and overall career advancement. Called the AAA Approach™, these three factors are as follows:

✔ Attitude

✔ Actions

✔ Achievement

When you add your newly acquired persuasion tools to my AAA Approach, it's full speed ahead. You become the driving force in your career.

## *The AAA Approach to a Promotion*

### Attitude

*Visualize Yourself Succeeding.* You deserve a satisfying and enriching career. Once you can visualize or see yourself in a successful role, obtaining the job you want or the promotion you want (enjoying the higher salary), you'll be on the path to obtaining that goal. Spend 10 minutes every day focusing on and visualizing your dreams coming true. Think about and then jot down the action steps that must be taken to achieve those goals. Before you know it, you'll have acquired many of these dreams and be setting new goals for yourself. A motivational book to start with is *Dare to Win* by Jack Canfield and Mark Victor Hansen (Berkley).

*You Can Obtain Any Career.* As long as you're willing to strive and work hard you can be anything that you want to be. On average, you're going to work for 11,000 days over your working lifetime. It's important that you feel that your work is meaningful, that it's satisfying, and that it enriches your life. This is our ultimate goal in trying to select a career and a job that really adds a wonderful dimension to your life.

*Don't Take a Promotion for Granted.* Assuming that because you have taken on responsibilities or filled in as the job became open will never guarantee your promotion. Act as if you *are* that manager. Perform at the higher level. Politics are at play. Get help from your allies. One woman, Cheryl, took over the newly created director's role. She performed it for six months until the final funding came through. Overconfident that she'd get the job, she went to the interview with a superior attitude. She ignored questions and just popped off with, "I won't do this, I will do that"—no preparation, no research to gain a more global insight into the job. It had to be her way . . . the old way. She had been considered the prime choice for the job.

But as the hiring process got under way, many outside candidates appeared with more diverse experiences. Cheryl's poor interview performance weakened her cause. Peggy, a well-prepared candidate, brought in an arsenal of tools. She used her contacts and got the inside scoop. Armed with a good 60 Second Sell, 5 Point Agenda, and past work examples, she impressed the hiring committee and got the job.

Prepare to earn your promotion. Take nothing for granted. Someone else can and will sneak up and grab the position if you don't work to earn the job.

*Understand Anxiety and Fears.*   Anytime we're trying to move forward or take on a new goal, we can feel a bit uncomfortable. To move to new heights, we've got to move outside of our comfort zone. That nervous anxiety and those little nagging fears you feel inside are really important reminders that you are achieving something different, that you're going forward, that you're taking a risk and trying. You may feel nervous about being different or doing something you haven't tried before, but keep focused. As long as you realize that anxiety and fear are part of the process of promotion and moving ahead, you'll be okay. Today's workplace is changing rapidly, requiring everyone to push themselves constantly so as to not get left behind.

*Create a Meaningful Job.*   You have so many options that you can pursue, so many different avenues and roads that you can follow. You'll be happiest if you select work you find interesting and that uses your most productive talents and abilities. On a daily basis, you should feel satisfied with the work you do. This should be your objective and goal. You deserve no less.

*Develop a Strong Work Ethic.*   There are two ways to approach your work. The first is a nine-to-five mentality: It's a job and a paycheck. The second is the career-with-a-future framework. When you do only what's required—you never volunteer, you never add more—the results are usually stagnation in your professional development. Top corporate executives continually tell me they need value-added employees—those who bring more to their jobs.

If you are recognized as a good, productive worker—one who is dependable, with initiative to improve and bring quality to the job—you'll stand out more to the upper echelon in your organization.

**CAREER COACH** *tip*

*An attitude and willingness to learn, adapt, and be flexible is critical to meeting the employer's changing needs.*

*Recognize Success in Others.*   Observing and applauding success in other people will not only make new friends for you but also expose you to new ideas and the possibilities for achievement that exist in others and in yourself. Write congratulatory notes when good things happen to other people: when they get promotions, win awards, or begin new jobs. Take the time to say, "Good going . . . congratulations!"

Identify people who recognize success and who try to achieve more in their own lives. Perhaps there's someone you admire—someone in your profession, someone in politics, someone who's successfully running a company. Get to know people you admire. These high achievers may become your mentors and eventually your friends. As you recognize success in others, you will begin to form patterns of building success within yourself: Mirroring the actions of others eliminates reinventing the wheel and produces great results. Most successful people are willing to help others—all you have to do is *ask.*

*Read Stories about Successful People.*   Study. How did the people you admire become successful? What are some of the things they've had to cope with to be able to achieve the success that they are enjoying today? The more you learn about what successful people have done, the more you'll understand that there are patterns toward success, patterns you should follow.

Many books have been written about success. A classic by Napoleon Hill is called *Think and Grow Rich.* Earl Nightingale, Brian Tracy, and many other authors have created audiotapes about success and success patterns. Concentrate on building success in your life by thinking about success, reading about it, learning about it, and then living it.

*Identify and Share Dreams Only with Enthusiastic Supporters.*   The world can be a very negative place. Oftentimes other people can become jealous of you and behave in a very petty way. They may feel threatened if they see you succeed beyond them. They may worry that you'll no longer be their friend or that you'll no longer be around to commiserate with them if you move on to something better. They will not encourage or praise your hard work or efforts to achieve more. Pick your supporters carefully. Identify people who will support your goals, be enthusiastic, and offer positive ideas and strategies to help you succeed.

*Listen to Motivational Tapes.*   You won't always have a friend on hand to offer the needed advice or success strategy. A powerful learning tool is available: motivational cassette tapes. My husband starts each morning listening to success tapes while he gets ready for work. He absorbs numerous ideas to help him perform better on the job. Use your commute time to "get the secrets of success" or learn the "communication tools" that will advance your career. Nightingale-Conant offers a terrific selection. (Earl Nightingale is my personal favorite. All of his work is inspiring.) You can get a free catalog by calling 800-525-9000.

*Develop a Passion to Achieve.*   Become enthusiastic about your own success. Take pride in doing a good job. Celebrate getting a raise, finishing a class, completing a project. Reward yourself, whether it be something simple like a cookie or a soda or something substantial like a new outfit. For big achievements, the reward should be something special— perhaps a vacation or even a new car. As you learn to set goals for yourself and achieve them, you must also relish your achievements. Always take time to reward yourself. The reward allows you to enjoy the fruits of your labor and formally acknowledges that you are succeeding toward the goals you set for yourself.

*Rise Above Office Politics.*   Nothing is more negative and can hurt you more than office politics. You may have been victimized by office politics, where the behavior around you is hurtful and petty and not controlled by management. Most offices have office politics, but some have run rampant in a destructive way that is hurting the organization and certainly damaging the productivity of the employees. You must set specific goals for yourself that say, "I'm going to rise above office politics." Don't gossip; don't malign anybody; don't put down other people; and, above all else, certainly don't sabotage someone else's career or their work, for this will surely come back and reflect poorly on you. I have found too many people who pay dearly when they immerse themselves in this minefield.

"As ye sow, so shall ye reap." This often proves true in life and your career. Managers should not allow such hurtful and petty behavior, and sometimes if a lot of politics are going on in your office, it might be a good idea to bring it up to upper management and say, "What can we do about this?"

I've long since held the assumption that the reason there's a lot of office politics going on, especially if it's bad gossip and maligning, is that the people simply aren't busy enough. Many managers agree—when you're active being highly productive, you gossip less because you don't have the time. You have things to do. You have end goals that you have to reach. Focus your time and energy on positive things. If you find you have an extra 15 minutes, instead of gossiping, use your 15 minutes in a productive effort. Many people have improved their careers by more constructively using little bits of time here and there. For a mountain of ideas, see the chart on page 162–165, "105 Great Ways to Use Fifteen Minutes for Productivity."

Personal attacks on you by other employees or nasty office politics may stem from people who feel threatened. They begin to think you may be more important than they are. For some reason, they feel jealous. You may have done something to create this. Examine your behavior to determine whether there may be some truth to such aspersions or if indeed it's just pettiness and jealousy. Sometimes the only answer to rampant and damaging office politics is a new work environment—a different place where employees function at a higher level and where productivity and organizational goals and satisfaction seem to be first in everybody's mind. Perhaps the grass will be greener somewhere else if the office politics have deteriorated to the point that you are unable to do a good job, excel, and succeed in positive ways. Be aware—office politics has destroyed more than one career. You are always in the driver's seat. Don't be victimized. Be smart about managing your career.

## Actions

*Explore Options.* There are so many opportunities available to you, so many options that your career can take, so many paths that you could follow. Take the time to explore your strengths, your values. Do some self-assessment. Perhaps you need to sit down and actually spend some time with a career counselor to help you focus on where you really want to go from here. As you manage your life, throughout your entire career there will be many new opportunities that can come your way. Some will be highly rewarding because you were insightful enough to take advantage of them. So always be on the lookout to explore new opportunities.

*Demonstrate Initiative.*   Many times it's your own suggestions that will make a project come off in a better light or that will improve a system or a process in your department. Be open to new ideas. Go to your boss when you have an idea. Offer many. The management might not take every one you put forth, but you will be seen as someone who shows initiative. Work on trying to do your very best at any job you have. Always be looking for ways to do things faster, more efficiently, more accurately, and in a more timely manner.

Volunteer to head a project. Offer to organize a committee or plan an event. Suggest that you'd be willing to research some potential equipment purchase and write up your recommendations. Volunteer to be the one to try out a new computer system. Assist in hiring new staff people. Train them. Use your initiative and efforts to expand your duties and skills and learn more on the job. Focus on improvements and, before you know it, your supervisor and your manager's supervisor will be noticing you.

*Develop an Action Plan.*   You must write out clear steps on how you're going to reach your goals. You can do this by having a weekly calendar in which you've set down your career goals and any action steps to be taken that week so you can keep working toward them. Perhaps you're going to make phone calls on your job search; you'd write those down to ensure it'll happen. Perhaps you're going to set up an informational interview; you'd want to note who you're going to call, when, and what you might say.

Action plans are absolutely necessary once you've determined what you want to do. Create a comprehensive, step-by-step plan listing all the necessary steps to reach your goal. *Written plans on how you'll reach your goals are imperative to your success.*

*Diversify Your Abilities.*   You'll encounter people who tend to pigeonhole you into one slot. The "Oh, you're a nurse, what could you possibly know about marketing?" attitude. You need to be active in broadening your knowledge base. Join organizations. Read various trade journals and books to spread out your knowledge and expertise. The new hiring philosophy values adaptable workers—those who are flexible and open to learning new things. Share new ideas. Be innovative. Think globally.

*Manage Your Time Well.*   We all have the same number of hours in each day. How you use them makes the important difference. Use a daily planner (e.g., Franklin Planner or DayTimer are good ones) to maximize your workday priorities. Plot out the time to devote to exciting projects, planning, and career pursuits. Not all employers allow you to participate in volunteer or association work during the job. Be sure to schedule those activities into your free time as needed. Using your planner and to-do lists can keep you efficient and more productive. In fact, on page 162–165 you'll find an entire list of activities you can do when you have 15 minutes to spare.

*Set Your Goals and Reevaluate Often.*   Don't let anybody else tell you what you should or shouldn't do. Set your own goals. Don't try to live through the dreams of your parents or your spouse or your friends. Only you know exactly what makes you happy. When you're choosing your career goals, you need to reevaluate them often, no less than once a year. Make sure your career is being managed, that it's kept in line with where you want it to be. The workplace keeps changing—so stay tuned to new and different trends. There may be a new skill you'd like to pick up. Perhaps you would like to do something different at the office. You might even go to the boss and suggest, "Oh, I'd like to write a newsletter!" There might be a new duty that you want to take on. Whatever your goals might be, continually reevaluate them so that at least once or twice a year you know exactly where you're going to go and how you're going to get there. Be sure to write down your goals. Writing seems to cement them, and it points out the steps needed to reach each one.

*Expect No One to Point the Way.*   Years ago, people would join a company and expect to be mentored, taken into a management training program, or taken under someone's wing, so to speak; their careers would blossom as they moved up the corporate ladder. That doesn't happen today. Your manager is too busy worrying about his or her job, trying to get the projects done on time, and reaching the goals set by management. Don't expect a company to take you by the hand and lead you up the promotion ladder. Don't expect a boss to invest that much time or energy in your career.

In the last few years, one important new reality we've learned is how very important it is for us to take on the responsibility of managing our own careers. You now are in the driver's seat. Only *you* can learn which way you've got to go or how you might want to succeed. You have to plan out the path for yourself. You can certainly get input from many good sources, but never expect someone else is going to do it for you or lead you by the hand.

*Network.*  Developing a lifelong list of contacts and professional associates will help your career immensely. Whether you're trying to solve a work problem, looking for a new job, or just trying to get new ideas in your field or area, being involved in a professional association makes a lot of sense to help manage your career. You can't expect to network only when you need a job; to be successful, networking should be an ongoing activity.

Be active in a professional association. Chair committees. Choose visible roles. Others will see you and get to know you. This is a great way to be the first person people think of when they are recruiting a new employee or manager for their organization. Many, many positions as officers or leaders in associations have led to great new jobs for those who have been actively involved over a long period of time. Build your network wisely. Offer help to those who ask, and develop new friendships with people whose careers you admire, those in places of authority to which you aspire.

If you are presently at a large organization, network internally. With thousands inside your company, many contacts can be made to help you perform better on the job and alert you to new opportunities in different divisions.

According to the Department of Labor, 63% of all jobs were found through contacts in the last year. Networking can be a key component when it's time to job hunt; therefore, always have a good network by being actively involved on a continual basis.

*Continually Improve Skills.*  The job market has gotten extremely competitive. The workplace now requires high-level skills in technology, writing, oral communication, interacting well with others, understanding budgets, and assimilating corporate goals. The best way to ensure career success is to continually learn new skills and improve the ones you've already acquired. Employers have stated that the number one skill they want to see from employees is good computer skills. The technology that has been running rampant in our country over the last decade has surely reshaped the workplace enormously. If you really want to advance your career, continually improve your computer systems and software usage skills. Be willing to learn new skills—advanced techniques in Microsoft

Word or a spreadsheet program such as Excel, for example. These can add greatly to the skills you'll have to offer your current employer or a future employer. If you do not possess a college degree, you should consider going to school and taking the types of specialty classes that are important to the field you're in—or one you desire to be in.

You can now pursue college degrees in nontraditional ways. There are many different options available to you for education and training. The old-fashioned correspondence courses now use videos, voice mail, e-mail, and actual classes over the Internet. Colleges refer to these as "distance learning" programs. This can be a very good option if you're a motivated student. You must pace yourself when undertaking such a program. Correspondence classes are available at many state colleges and universities throughout the country. Simply call and ask for the distant-learning department to find out more about what might be available to work with your schedule.

There are college extension or satellite programs that have all kinds of options available, with bachelor's and master's degrees being taught in the evenings, on weekends, and in accelerated executive programs. Use your investigative skills to determine what's available in your area. For information about college programs, contact the academic adviser or the admissions officer at any college or university. These individuals can provide you with a catalog or manual that tells you about these kinds of specialty programs. For personal and professional growth, obtain more training and acquire more skills—through college or university classes, seminars taught by business groups, your corporate training department, or maybe your professional association.

Additionally, community and technical colleges offer a broad range of courses and specialty programs that are relatively inexpensive and often necessary to move in a new direction. Many times, one or two courses is all you need to master a new skill.

In addition to taking classes, there are other options. You could read a book. If you devoted just 30 or 40 minutes a day, you could read 24 books in the course of a year. These books could teach you many things: how to be a better manager, how to hire people, how to cope with difficult people. You could learn how to provide better customer service, how to improve sales, how to enhance marketing techniques, how to write press releases, or how to develop a complex budget. The list is endless. These skills can be self-taught. People read books every day to learn new things.

You could get involved in a volunteer organization taking on a new project. Working in a community group or an association can be a terrific way to perfect new skills that you don't have the opportunity to pick up at your current place of employment. In fact, many people get management skills by volunteering, which provides the experience they need to finally penetrate the ranks of management.

Computer skills, as I've mentioned before, are really vital, so I firmly recommend that you continually work on yours. Try to improve your proficiency with the programs that you use in your office. You might want to expand and learn a new application that you could use if you moved to a different position or organization.

What are the skills that employers say they want? Well, I just mentioned one. Computer skills are tops, but another important skill that you could be working on improving is communication—being able to converse clearly and articulate ideas. Public speaking is an important skill; in fact, one-third of everybody in America is petrified of public speaking, so that might be something you want to work on.

Good written communication skills are becoming essential for a society driven by technology, knowledge, and information. Devote time to improve your report writing, maybe even contribute an article to your newsletter. Employers value managerial skills. Today's style is to act more like a coach and certainly less like a dictatorial boss. The coach sets out a game plan and allows the individuals to take responsibility for how they're going to get the job done. You'll need to learn this newer management style. You'll need to encourage accountability and foster individual autonomy if you are going to be the kind of manager that is vital to your company's future success.

Many top CEOs and presidents have reported that the one skill they wish more managers had was a good understanding of how budgets work. They want you to understand that the financial picture is the bottom line. Whether an organization is nonprofit or commercial, everything comes down to dollars and cents. Ask knowledgeable people to help you have a better understanding of your company's budgets. Perhaps you could sit down with someone in the accounting office who could actually show you how the credit, debit, liabilities, and expenses are handled so that you'll understand how to create and manage a budget of your own. If you already operate a budget, be sure to look for ways to cut costs. Upper management values leaders who make the most of the resources they have available.

Another skill that employers really prize is the ability to prioritize your workload and be productive. This requires good time-management skills on your part to define tasks, manage projects, and meet your deadlines.

For managers, delegation is also essential. Include your boss when setting goals to make sure that you both have the same priorities and that you're working on the projects in the order that your boss sees as most important.

Teamwork and the ability to accomplish work and projects with others are essential skills to develop. Today's changing workplace has employers seeking employees who truly are team players.

Finally, many senior managers include sales and marketing savvy and an emphasis on customer service as keys to success. Everyone needs to understand what it is you're selling, be it a service, a product, or a mission objective. Additionally, you must be able to communicate and be a promoter of that service or product, telling other people about your company, becoming a referral source, so to speak.

In terms of customer service, you may have internal customers, as, for example, when you are serving other departments. If you are in, say, accounting, the various departments for whom you produce financial reports are your customers. If you're in the sales department, your customer may be the person who actually buys the product. Everyone inside the company needs to be service-oriented. Quality and service are the new standards that are reshaping today's workplace, and they're going to be important skills that you must practice on a daily basis.

*Add Value.*    Senior management now looks for people who add value to the company, process, or team. Such people are deemed "assets." Focus on adding value by continually examining how you are taking charge of your job and showing initiative to do it better.

*Be Flexible.*    A competitive advantage you can develop is to become flexible and adaptable to meeting the employer's changing needs. The rate of change in the workplace is incredibly fast and growing exponentially. Many people feel insecure and resist change, but employers continue to seek out and promote those who've demonstrated that they are flexible and who easily adapt to change.

*Develop a Great Resumé and Live It.*    Your career is developed over your lifetime. The decisions you make today, the things you do, the projects you work on, will affect how your career is shaped in the years to come. Therefore, work on actively developing a great resumé.

Careers come in a gradual progression, brick by brick. You can't expect to start at the top. But do have a clear idea of how to get there if the top is indeed where you wish to be.

You need to make career choices that allow you to take on a leadership role, improve the department, add to the overall system. Always look for ways that you might be able to save money or improve a process, system, or a project so later on you'll have noted results from your efforts that you can report to future employers. Remember, it's those initiatives, the little bit extra that you do, the personal excellence you bring to the job, and the activities you take on that allow you to develop a great resumé. Once you start living this success-orientation philosophy, you'll see terrific opportunities come your way.

## Achievement

*Dream Big.* Ted Turner once said, "The bigger the dreams the better. I set more goals than I could possibly ever achieve in one lifetime. Then I try like heck to reach 'em." It's important to realize that only with dreams can we move forward. Once we achieve a dream, we must set new goals for ourselves. In Ted Turner's case, he started out owning one television station, but then he built it into WTBS, one of the biggest television stations in the entire country. His cable channel evolved into a broadcasting empire. His news channel (CNN) is one of the biggest cable channels in the entire world. The activity of setting goals for yourself is rooted in your dreams. Set goals, no matter how high, for whatever it is that you want. Make sure some are a little out of your reach. When you finally get there—and you will get there—go out and set new goals: bigger . . . better . . . higher. Write down your dreams and goals. Define how you will know when you've achieved this success. In other words, state the dream and define the evidence that will acknowledge you have "made it." For example, if you're telling someone, "I want to be famous," then you must define, "What will fame look like to me?" The answer might be, "I'll know I'm famous when I'm on the cover of *People* magazine." Well, you might want to have a few other goals, too, but that is one measuring stick. Suppose you say, "Well, I want to be successful." Then you must elaborate and determine how you will know if you've succeeded. Many people say, "Well, I'll have a house or I'll have a car." Be specific. What kind of house? How big? What kind of neighborhood? Where will it be located? And what kind of car? Do you dream of a Lexus or would you be happy just to get a Saturn that's brand new? Set these goals and, when you reach them, dream bigger dreams for yourself. Dreams are what make life worthwhile. They give us the passion to get up in the morning, to go to work, and to be excited about living, about our work, and about the jobs we want to do. That enthusiasm will spread throughout not only your job, but your company. It will result in you being a person to whom others are drawn. People will want to come and talk to you as you become recognized as an important leader.

*Victims Always Fail.*   The world is full of dysfunctional people and dysfunctional situations. If you're looking for someone to blame for the reasons that you aren't more successful, you need to stop and take a real close look in the mirror. Blaming others puts you in a victim role, and when you're in a victim role, you will always fail. Victims spend all their time blaming and no time looking for solutions or options to their problems. A senior executive at one of America's top telecommunications companies offered this insight: "During management meetings we often ask, 'Is he or she part of the solution or part of the problem?' An employee's efforts are either one or the other." You must operate as a winner. Explore options. Seek alternatives. Take responsibility. You must think about how you can improve your situation. Bad things happen to great people. Job layoffs come, mergers happen, and through no fault of your own you might find yourself without a job. A new manager might come in tomorrow, and a promotion that you were almost guaranteed can float away and no longer be yours when the new manager decides you aren't the person to do that job.

You must take responsibility for the life you create. And, above all else, avoid "black cloud" people. These are those doomsayers who walk around and seem to attract bad things to them. They use excuses—"The boss doesn't like me," "I got sick," or "I don't have any time to go to class to learn how." "Black cloud" people can find more circumstances to prevent themselves from succeeding. "Black cloud" people need to be avoided. As we said earlier, surround yourself with people who think about success, focus on success, are supportive, and point out good options when you're faced with difficult choices.

*Strive for Excellence.*   Above all else, do quality work. No matter what your occupation or what field you pursue, being known as a good worker will ensure that when it's time to look for a job other employers will want to hire you. The better performance ensures your future job security.

You don't have to put in much more effort to be viewed as a good worker as opposed to only an average worker. A recent employment study showed that it required only 2% more effort to be deemed a good worker versus just average. Use little pockets of time, an extra 15 minutes here or there, to improve the quality of your work. Make suggestions. Take pride in what you do. Proofread. Check it over. Make sure things are accurate. Know when your deadlines are and plan your time to be sure you can make it when it's necessary. Go the extra mile and put in the time when the work demands it or the employer needs the extra help.

Strive for excellence for no one other than yourself. Set high standards and make sure you live by them. When you strive for excellence, others will recognize that you're a person who really is a contributor, someone they definitely want on their team. Striving to do quality work will ensure your career mobility, whether you move on to new jobs or are sought out for promotions in the organization you work for now. Secondarily, you must gravitate toward your strengths. When you are using the skills and the special talents that are unique to you, the ones that make you feel as if it's not work at all, it becomes easy to be good at whatever you choose to do. If you gravitate toward your strengths, toward the natural abilities you have, and if you develop these skills that you enjoy doing, then you'll achieve even higher success. When you're enjoying your work, you spend more time reading, you spend more time learning, and you'll spend more time trying to achieve and excel. Those activities will lead to the ultimate achievement: reaching the goal that you've set for yourself—a promotion. You can accomplish an entire career full of promotions and advancements, taking you anywhere you want to go.

*Record Your Achievements.*   The Productivity Monitor (Chapter 4) is designed to allow you an easy way to track your daily wins, successes, and accomplishments. I recommend you develop the major contributions into your resumé. The Monitor tracks your progress and is a valuable tool to influence promotion and raise decisions. You'll want to be sure you add to your Monitor *every month.*

## PRODUCTIVITY MONITOR

**January** _____

_____

_____

**February** _____

_____

**March** _____

_____

**April** _____

_____

**May** _____

_____

**June** _____

_____

**July** _____

_____

**August** _____

_____

**September** _____

_____

**October** _____

_____

**November** _____

_____

_____

**December**

_____

_____

_____

**MAJOR RESUMÉ ACCOMPLISHMENTS FOR THE YEAR**

- _____

- _____

- _____

- _____

- _____

- _____

Now you've gotten the complete AAA Approach (_Attitude, Actions, Achievement_) to manage your professional growth and move your career in any direction you prefer.

# _Moving into Management_

A top executive at a Fortune 100 company offered a candid view of the over 100,000 employees who worked for the organization. He said, "Many people say they want to be in management, but few earn the right." He noted that today's workplace requires leaders who possess the experience and behavioral traits needed to continue the company's success. He cited the need to be able to get along with people, and the ability to get things done in a team. You as an individual must add value to the whole.

This executive (whose career path to the top is one most people would envy) prescribed the ideal for the manager he wants to hire or promote— the manager who will meet today's and tomorrow's business challenges:

The new manager must be an excellent performer with high ethical standards. The person must be committed to the company's principals, goals, and standards. Quality must be an important priority. The manager must treat people with respect and trust and earn the same for himself or herself from those he or she works with. He or she must promote teamwork and empower others. The person needs to demonstrate innovation and seek intellectual growth and learning. You must share information, be an open communicator and, above all, listen.

These are the new criteria by which his company judges employees for management and advancement roles.

Do you have what it takes to be a manager? Here are 10 important questions to ponder.

## Quiz: 10 Ways to Determine If You Could Be a Good Manager

### HAVE YOU GOTTEN MORE TRAINING?

Getting additional education is the fastest way to move ahead. Debra, a hospital medical records specialist, dreamed of being a manager. She went to college at night and sacrificed six years of hard work to get her bachelor's degree. She took out student loans and financed the rest from her paycheck. When she combined her work experience and new diploma, she landed a healthcare manager position at Pacific Medical with a $7,000 salary increase. Thomas, a full-time worker at a local bank, went to graduate school for four years to earn his MBA. It was a continuous challenge and sacrifice to give up most of his other activities as he held a job while he took the courses. Upon graduation, his aggressive job search landed him a terrific marketing position as a manager for an emerging-technology company.

Obtaining a degree is not always necessary to move ahead, but getting essential skills to do the job is. Employers seek managers with excellent written and oral communication skills. Supervisors excel on their job when they've learned how to effectively manage staff and workloads. To get started, sign up for classes on supervision and communication skills. National seminar programs such as Career Track or Fred Pryor have one-day programs. You can also check with your local colleges. More training is likely needed for you to move ahead.

### HAVE YOU COACHED OTHERS?

Being able to motivate other employees and oversee their work are critical managerial skills. Debra, our hospital records specialist, also spent a lot of her spare time on her computer. She enjoyed teaching others and frequently offered to show staff how to use the company's complex systems. She volunteered to train newly hired people on the computer and other office procedures. This gave her exposure to management that wasn't defined in her job.

Another avenue for you to gain some supervisory experience is to offer to oversee temporary workers or head up a committee or project. Ask yourself: "Do I give clear directions? Do I look to solve problems instead of assigning blame? Do I check to see that the work is progressing correctly and in a timely fashion? Do I recognize that there are multiple ways to get a job done well? Do I easily encourage people?" These are important tasks necessary to succeed.

### CAN YOU DELEGATE AND MAKE GOOD DECISIONS?

Both abilities—delegation and decision making—are necessary, as a manager must assign work, plan projects, and make numerous choices daily. Thomas, our MBA pursuer, was the team leader for a graduate school market research project. He alone was responsible for getting every team member to perform his or her part on a tight time schedule. He helped solve problems, assigned the tasks, and in a fair way utilized each member's individual strengths and talents. Coordinating such a massive project really honed his project management abilities.

Practice implementing both these decision-making and delegation skills on your job, at home, or in community activities. Become active in your local association and take on leadership roles. That's where many people get the key supervisory experience that prevented them from joining management ranks in the past. Learn how to give assignments to others, providing the time and resources necessary to successfully complete the tasks.

### DO YOU TAKE ON MORE RESPONSIBILITY
### WHILE DEMONSTRATING INITIATIVE AND PRODUCTIVITY?

America's workplace is being swept with continuous downsizings and streamlining to increase productivity. It requires that today's manager be independent and able to make significant contributions. Do you make a habit of asking for more work and expanding the scope of your current job? Do you contribute new ideas to improve your department or office? Can you easily adjust to change?

Jeanne, an executive secretary for a large manufacturer, volunteered for a big project: planning a major company conference. Here was her chance to really show them what she could do. Jeanne surpassed her boss's expectations by planning and pulling off a highly successful event. She efficiently organized and procured food, lodging, and speakers, saving her company a significant amount of money. Top executives took notice, and within three months she was promoted into management.

## HOW STRONG ARE YOUR COMMUNICATION SKILLS?

Employers value good communicators, as they are essential in developing a productive workforce. Learn to listen, explain clearly, and give understandable directions. Today's communication skills mean utilizing technology—computers, Internet, voice mail, teleconferencing—to transmit information. Both oral and written skills are paramount to your management success. Practice speaking and facilitating meetings. Join Toastmasters. Volunteer to serve on office committees and be an active participant. You can improve your written skills by writing more reports, articles for newsletters, composing correspondence, or taking classes.

## ARE YOU A GOOD LISTENER?

Employees like managers who ask for and listen to their ideas and suggestions. They feel more understood when you listen attentively to their requests or needs or while they outline a problem. Practice learning to let a person explain, while you nod and take in what's being said. Do not interrupt. Managers need to allow others to express themselves completely, no matter how hurried or pressured you may be. You need to hear everything, then formulate your response after you've interpreted what they are saying. Be sure your responses are appropriate and that others see the communication and interaction with you in a positive light.

## HAVE YOU OBSERVED AND EMULATED GOOD MANAGERS?

Moving into management requires different attitudes, perspectives, interpersonal skills, and a professional presentation. Study managers you respect. How assertive are they? What abilities identify them as good managers? How do they think and make decisions? Emulate their strengths to develop your own skills. Learn how to handle problems by watching how they resolve tricky issues. Ask for their recommendations for books on how to motivate others and manage workloads. People always work hardest and are most loyal to managers who praise and reward their good work. Develop that pattern.

Pay particular attention to the clothing you select to wear. You must look and act the part of a manager to be recognized as someone who's serious and promotable.

Customer service is essential to be seen as management (or upper management) material. Follow the lead of the most admired managers you know. Pay particular attention to what they do and say and how they treat customers. Show the same positive, service-oriented, problem-solver attitude toward all those with whom you interact.

## DO YOU OPERATE USING HIGH PROFESSIONAL STANDARDS AND ETHICS?

Upper management will seek out managers who display high moral standards. Do you respect other employees? Are you careful not to offend anyone? Are you sensitive to diversity issues from workers that may have a different cultural background than yours? Do you treat everyone as an equal and harbor no prejudices against minorities, the disabled, or homosexuals? Are you careful not to use terminology that others might deem offensive? Do you treat all people fairly? In today's workplace you must show a high level of integrity and avoid actions or words that could be seen as sexual harassment or discriminatory.

## DO YOU HAVE THE SELF-CONFIDENCE TO MAKE GOOD CHOICES AND ASSERT YOURSELF?

To become a manager, you must take action and plan. Work hard to improve professionally. Your self-concept must allow you to envision yourself as a manager and to act like one long before you're likely to move ahead.

Debra, our medical records specialist, found that her coworkers at the hospital disagreed with her efforts to gain more schooling. They didn't cheer her on. They told her she was wasting her time and working too hard. Debra realized the truth—if she became a manager, she'd no longer be like them. Once she stopped listening to all the naysayers it became easier to achieve success. She didn't let others dissuade her with their comments like "You work too hard" or "Why do you bother?"

Jeanne, our executive secretary, knew she could plan a successful event. She used lunch hours and some time at home to determine what had been done before so she could determine what the group's preferences were. She negotiated the catering and accommodations with a tone of authority. She not only saved money, but added to the creativity that made the event memorable for everyone there—particularly upper management.

Both Debra's and Jeanne's extra efforts moved their careers along.

**The formula to move into a management position requires a skill set of abilities:**

Decision making

Delegation

Communications

Good listener

Initiative

Productivity

Results

Coaching

High standards

Ethics

Quality work

## CAN YOU HANDLE PRESSURE DEADLINES AND SET AND MEET GOALS?

The higher you go, the more stress and pressure you'll likely encounter. You need to develop coping mechanisms that let you handle the challenge without burning out. Regular exercise is an important stress reliever.

Develop good time-management skills. When you plan projects, allow for some temporary setbacks. Develop a timeline that outlines the tasks on a spreadsheet. As your workload (and the number of people under you) increases you need to become well organized to ensure you meet company goals. Having to put out small fires gives you the foundation to deal more effectively with the bigger problems as they arise.

## 105 Great Ways to Use 15 Minutes for Productivity

Since today's corporate yardstick is productivity, it makes sense to utilize your time wisely. Fifteen minutes here or there can add up to big, noticeable improvements and changes down the line. This list offers 105 ways you can improve your performance—and results—when time is short.

1. Plan out weekly schedule.
2. Write a letter.
3. Plan a project.
4. Proofread your work.
5. Open the mail.
6. Listen to your voice mail messages.
7. Read your e-mail.
8. Help a customer.
9. Answer the phone.
10. Organize your workstation.
11. Show someone how to use a piece of equipment.
12. Help a coworker with something.
13. Organize to-do tasks; prioritize work.

14. Have discussions with individual staff members.

15. Return calls.

16. Review reports.

17. Write status reports.

18. Create spreadsheets.

19. Update memos on issue items.

20. File.

21. Call a client.

22. Market to a new client.

23. Copy something.

24. Print out something from the computer.

25. Review a tutorial for software.

26. Set up lunch with clients or prospects.

27. Read the *Wall Street Journal.*

28. Read trade publications or journals.

29. Set up new files on Excel.

30. Organize files.

31. Work on a section of employee appraisal.

32. Reconcile an account or budget.

33. Update procedures for office systems.

34. File management reports.

35. Read a computer book to help solve problems.

36. Make a list of projects that would help the company.

37. Make a list of projects that would help your department.

38. Think about how to reorganize your department to make it more efficient.

39. Talk with other managers about problems.

40. Brainstorm solutions to problems.

41. Have a 15-minute meeting to discuss problems.

42. Think of ways to improve job efficiency.

43. Talk to the boss about new ideas.

44. Add more detail when writing reports.

45. Call customers and ask for feedback on how the company is doing.

46. Listen to a cassette tape on a work subject.

47. Learn a new software program over three months.

48. Break down a big task into smaller components.

49. Practice learning a foreign language.

50. Learn to be a better salesperson.

51. Learn a new skill, such as selling, hiring, negotiating, managing.

52. Organize your errand list.

53. Separate short- and long-term duties.

54. Print out reports.

55. Research client questions.

56. Outline a response to a letter.

57. Read an article or newsletter.

58. List five new prospective clients.

59. Refer to a reference book to clarify procedure.

60. Prioritize work for the day.

61. Fax something.

62. Respond to e-mail.

63. Read memos.

64. Send e-mail asking nonurgent questions or initiating requests.

65. Coordinate a meeting.

66. Write an agenda for a meeting.

67. Distribute reports.

68. Delegate tasks to others.

69. Throw away unnecessary papers.

70. Set up appointments.

71. Write project updates for the boss.

72. Go through active files and finish one thing.

73. Talk to another team member.

74. Redo a form that doesn't work or looks sloppy.

75. Set up appointments.

76. Discuss a new project with coworkers.

77. Call existing customers to thank them for business.

78. Review/analyze customer base.

79. Read the competition's product information.

80. Check on and, if necessary, order supplies.

81. Update database.

82. Update your mailing and address lists.

83. Back up computer files.

84. Update your Rolodex.

85. Organize or schedule preliminaries on a future meeting, conference, or event.

86. Make travel reservations.

87. List areas for improvement.

88. Tell someone he or she has done a good job.

89. Review goals.

90. Think of a more productive way to do a task.

91. Organize your paperwork.

92. Think about ideas to lower costs.

93. Write a thank-you note.

94. Distribute mail.

95. Write a memo to the boss praising an employee.

96. Double-check numbers.

97. Write a memo.

98. Study new policies and procedures.

99. Do data entry.

100. Return a phone call.

101. Go through a box and pull out hot items.

102. Check in with assistant, ask about his or her workload and listen for problems.

103. Talk to bosses about management concerns.

104. Read mail.

105. Document procedures to pass on to others to avoid continuous training.

A time management seminar might be a good way for you to learn how to maximize and control your time and personal productivity. A good one to take is Franklin Quest's full-day Time Quest Seminar ($199; 800-901-1776). It comes with their wonderful Daily Planner to organize both your professional and personal life.

## When the Best Way to Get Ahead Is to Move On

You may do everything possible and still a promotion may elude you. Less-qualified people may move up. Less-competent or docile people may be the ones who get promoted. Those less driven and less innovative may get the promotion you are hoping for. Sometimes promotions don't seem fair. When this happens, as it may, you need to make appropriate career choices that are right for you.

Opportunities in large organizations where promotions used to be very common and regular are disappearing fast. In the past, most promotions involved jobs in middle management. These are the very jobs that have been downsized and eliminated. Today and in the future, more people will find themselves in organizations where there is nowhere to go.

If you feel stymied in your progress, take a long, thorough look at what you want. One client, Mark, a state budget analyst, had this to say:

> I got so frustrated with my department and bosses when I couldn't get promoted. I was shocked when someone took me aside one day and said, "Unless you change your behavior and attitude, you'll go no far-ther." It was demoralizing, but also eye-opening. I got frightened and defensive, but I did think it over. He gave me so many examples— "You never work extra, you don't demonstrate leadership, never vol-unteer for committees, you're negative and express strong opinions that distress other employees." The person told me in a coaching, helpful way but I still felt devastated. I guess when it came to a pro-motion, I just felt I deserved it.

"Entitlement" is the syndrome that many people operate under. They justify their wants with an "I deserve it" attitude. Many managers iden-tify this as a serious transition they face in shaping their workforce for tomorrow.

Career progression is a series of choices, behaviors, performances, and opportunities. At different times in your life you will be at different professional stages. In your 20s you're learning about fields and getting those initial breaks. You feel the sky's the limit.

In your 30s people realize exactly what sacrifices (the long hours, travel requirements, possibly graduate school, relocations) go hand in hand with moving ahead. Many make significant changes in their 40s to put the family first. By 50, some are more interested in just maintaining the status quo than pushing harder in their career.

Mark's examination of his behavior and attitude was the first step toward professional change. To begin with, he got angry and mailed out resumés—he even got a job offer with another state agency. It was a good opportunity—a challenging position setting up a new division. But he was also realistic and knew it would require long hours for an indefinite period of time. When we discussed the offer together, he was hesitant. I told Mark, "Career choices are just that—choices. You create your life. You must decide based on your values and what you honestly want for yourself." With three small children at home, the long hours would keep him away a great deal. How "hard" you wish to work is a choice only you can make. But I've not seen too many people who rose through the ranks working only 40 hours a week. As you get past the first management levels, the jobs become increasingly stressful. The higher you go, the more pressure you often are under.

Tina was a program manager and had a good job within a large scientific organization that had 25,000 employees. She told me that since it was a very male-dominated field she had been unable to get a promotion. We discussed the facts and I encouraged Tina to investigate other departments in her organization. Two months later she saw a new job in the training and program development area. She applied, sailed through the interview, and easily persuaded them to offer her the job. Tina was pleased and went to her current boss and told him about the new position. She did not get the reaction she'd hoped for. He wished her luck and said he thought of her as a friend and would miss seeing her every day. He promised that they'd "do lunch" to stay in touch. Tina came to see me immediately afterward. She said, "I got the job," and burst into sobs. She loved the current department and its people—but they hadn't countered with an offer to keep her. She said, "That's what they usually do," and cried more.

I listened and sympathized with her situation. Once she got over the hurt she felt, we discussed the new position. It was definitely a promotion—a very nice promotion. It sounded as though it would be an interesting job. The big drawback was that she'd spent 11 years in her current department. She had established many good relationships with the people. I pointed out that moving to another area just a block or two away was not like moving to Outer Mongolia. With effort, she could maintain those relationships. The most influential factor in the end was that this promotion paid $5,000 more. As a single parent, she felt that the additional money would provide many extras and allow her to qualify for a remodeling loan to update her modest house. She took the job. She stayed a year and did very well. Thirteen months after she'd moved on, a new division head position was created in her old department. She was recruited back with yet another promotion and salary increase.

Sometimes you may need to look beyond your immediate area, as Tina did. My clients have moved to other departments inside their companies and seen their careers bloom. Whether it's because of renewed interest in your job, a different manager, or new people observing you and listening to your ideas, a new area can take your career out of neutral.

For many people, the very best way to move ahead will be to move on to a completely new and different employer. According to the Small Business Administration, two out of every three new jobs created in America in the last year were with small employers (less than 100 employees). In tiny organizations, the only place to go is often somewhere else. For example, Tim was an accountant for a small company. As the company grew into a $3 million per year entity, his duties increased. So did the hours. He averaged 70 to 80 hours a week and could not get the owners to give him a staff person or much of a raise. He wanted the title of "controller," which was the job he was doing. The owner, fearful that he'd want too much money, kept refusing. Tim looked at his options. Moving on seemed the only solution. We worked on his persuasion skills, and he quickly got hired as an assistant controller, with better benefits and an $11,000 salary boost. Just recently, he was promoted to controller.

Decisions on promotions—getting one or not getting one—will most likely be the most influential factor in your career decisions. Always seek advice from respected colleagues and senior managers. A qualified career counselor can offer objective insight and might be a worthwhile investment of time and money to help you gain a clear perspective. But, in the end, the career you create is your own. If you don't like your situation or what you are doing, you *can* change it.

# *Making the Most of Your Current Job*

When Mark, our budget analyst who was frustrated about not being promoted, chose not to move on to the new job, he began to behave differently at the job he had. After a couple of coaching sessions, he put new energy into his current job and took a better attitude toward work. He volunteered to be on a committee. Since he enjoyed the computer, he worked with a couple of staff people to teach them some more sophisticated computer application processes. He made himself into a kind of internal technical support resource. Mark had truly changed. Eventually, his managers acknowledged that it wasn't a short-term, but a permanent, improvement.

Fourteen months after our first meeting, Mark got a promotion. He told me, "You know, when *I* changed, the job seemed to get better. I have been given a great deal more computer systems to oversee. I really enjoy it. It's so easy for me. I never thought I'd be happy here, but I admit to you, Robin, now I am."

Mark learned some valuable lessons about achieving career satisfaction:

✔ You can define your own work tasks.

✔ Using your natural talents (often viewed by yourself as "easy work"), you can ask for and develop the more interesting parts of your job.

✔ A positive, cooperative attitude increases your ability to work and get things done as part of a team (required management skills).

✔ The grass may be pretty green in your current job if you apply yourself and challenge yourself to find areas for improvement.

✔ Volunteer to take on new duties and/or get duties reassigned to try out new skills or work in capacities that you find more enjoyable.

When you care about your job, it shows. You have more pride and you produce high-quality results. Your attitude and willingness to adapt and change, along with some extra effort, can produce the biggest change of all: turning your current job into one much more to your liking.

# HOW TO MAKE MORE $MONEY$!

*Carpe Diem!*
*(Seize the Day!)*

Y ou should be paid what you are worth. Most people will see the biggest financial increases when they change jobs or get a promotion. Others will be successful when they ask for and obtain a raise. There are proven strategies and guidelines that will aid you in obtaining your true financial worth. But before you begin, you must *know* that you are worth it. You must be confident of your value. Expect that you will be paid fairly for your contributions. Your belief and attitude will directly impact the outcome of any financial negotiations you undertake.

**Believe you are worth more; then back it up with facts, documentation, and accomplishments.**

The one area in which you need to be the most persuasive to get excellent results is salary negotiations. You can use tools such as the Hiring Chart or the Performance Chart. The Salary Extractor is a very clever and useful tool to determine the real range an employer will pay for the job to be done. You must use these tools with a solid attitude, confident that you know your value. As we learned in Chapter 5, Evian bottled water is *perceived* to be better water. Because of that perception, $150 million was spent last year by individuals who wanted that "better value." Your perception of yourself must be put in a similar light. You are like Evian—a perceived better value and thus worth more than others. *Perceived value:* It's what you establish in the employer's mind that determines the dollars offered. Employers may not go as high as you want, but you'll convince them you are worth being paid as much as their budgets allow.

# *Salary Negotiations*

Men and women approach salary negotiations quite differently. If I were to call a man and a woman with similar backgrounds and offer them the same job, typically the end results would be amazingly different. I've confirmed this observation over the years with clients, employers, and seminar participants. Here's how the job offer conversation usually goes.

June, the CFO of a medium-size company, calls to offer Donna the job as her controller.

JUNE: Well, Donna, I'm happy to offer you the job.

DONNA: Great!

JUNE: We're pleased. I can offer you $63,000 to start, plus we have an annual bonus that's determined in part by individual performance, and the other half is based on the company's year-end results. Of course, we have a complete medical and retirement plan. I do hope you'll take the job.

DONNA: Oh yes, I'm really excited.

JUNE: When can you start?

DONNA: Today's the 13th. . . . Is the 1st okay with you?

JUNE: That works. Personnel will call you about all our benefits and mail along new employee forms. See you on the 1st.

Now let's play out this scenario based on June, the CFO, selecting Allen, a male candidate for the controller's job.

JUNE: Well Allen, I'm happy to offer you the job.

ALLEN: That's terrific, June, I'm very interested in the position.

JUNE: I can offer you our full benefits package and starting salary of $63,000. Additionally, we have an annual bonus that's determined in part by individual performance, and the other half is based on company year-end performance. I hope you'll take the job.

ALLEN: Like I said, June, I'm very interested. Can we arrange a time for me to come in and meet with you tomorrow to talk about it?

JUNE: Sure—4 P.M. would be good for me.

ALLEN: I'll be there. By the way, June, I know you had a lot of strong contenders. Can I ask why you selected me?

JUNE: Certaly. I felt that it was three things. You have strong computer netrking and systems experience—it takes forever to get someone to speed on that. Your old boss attested to your reengineering ai productivity enhancements, plus he told me you were one of the st negotiators he'd ever seen. Those areas are all strengths wneed to complement our team.

ALLEN: Well, tnk you for the assessment! I really feel I could do an excellent jobr you. I look forward to tomorrow.

Allen used the ixt 24 hours constructively. He was a client, so we conversed about hiapproach and strategy. He prepared a Hiring Chart, had a salary surveylus determined his quantifying points.

He arrived at Jun office a few minutes early, and she gave him a tour and introduced hn to more of the staff. Then they went to her office and she closed the do.

ALLEN: Well June, I1 impressed with you—I think we'd work well together. The comany is headed into a growth phase. I love those challenges. Overal everything looks pretty good. But considering my strengths—I'vgot 13 years in the accounting field, and you noted the strong coputer systems and negotiation skills I'd bring to the job—I though your salary offer for someone with my background was a little lw.

JUNE: [*After a long, thoughtful pause . . .*] Well, Allen, we certainly want to be competitiv and get the best possible people for the job. Exactly what where ju thinking?

ALLEN: Well, June, I broight in this survey from the American Institute of CPAs. You'll se it shows the salary range for this size company to be between $50,000 to $80,000. [*He hands her the survey.*] It seems to m that my talents and accomplishments and the fact that I know yoir computer network system should move me pretty far up the scale. Here's a chart I drew up with your major needs and my contributions for you to review. [*Allen hands June this Hiring Chart he created.*]

JUNE: [*To herself, June thought, $80,000 is out of our range. I might get a few dollars from the overage fund. I wonder if he'll go for $70,000. That's about tops I think I could spend. Darn, I don't want to lose him. Well, I'll offer our best and see how it goes. Maybe something else can be thrown in to tip the scales.*] Allen, you are surely above average. But with our current budget situa-

## ALLEN MCCLEARY'S HIRING CHART

| Needs | Contributions |
|---|---|
| **CPA** | **13 years in the accounting fiel5 as a controller for a midsize company.** |
| **Computer Network Systems** | **LAN expertise and programng capability in FORTRAN. Developed corpate network and integrated entire systemProvided technical support to all depaments. Implemented computerized GL syem, inventory, and billing system. Eliminatd two full-time staff positions as a result, wile increasing overall productivity.** |
| **Reengineering** | **Team leader of company'sntire reengineering efforts. Costs decreasd by 7%, productivity enhancements incrsed by 30%.** |
| **Vendor/Negotiations** | **Negotiated over 400 corracts, obtaining better prices, discounts,nd terms. Savings surpassed $100,000.** |
| **Bank Relations** | **Coordinated cash manjement and negotiated loans and lines ofredit on cyclical business to maintain song cash flow.** |

tion, there's no use wasting time. I think $?,000 is the top offer we could make. Your bonus would run $12000 to $18,000 on top of that, and I would include you in this yei's bonuses. Is that doable?

ALLEN: Well, I really had $75,000 in mind.

JUNE: Honestly, Allen, I just don't have it. Isthere anything else? We have an excellent profit-sharing plan andfull medical benefits.

ALLEN: [*Thinking awhile before answering. . .*] Well June, let's see. Personnel told me your standard vacatioı is one week, then two weeks after three years, and three weeks after five. Isn't that right?

JUNE: Yes.

ALLEN: Well, each year my wife and I like to visit our family in California over Christmas. That takes a week. I have three weeks' vacation now, and I'd miss those summer trips if I had only one week the first few years I was here. Let me propose this, then, as an option. I'll get two weeks vacation at the start, then the third week after my second year. The base salary would be $71,000. If you can make it a package, I'd be pleased with that and glad to accept your offer.

JUNE: *[She thought it over to herself: Personnel hates it when you change the vacation, but I probably can get them to okay it. Allen has the background I need, and both his former employers loved him. I'll make it work out. I can't lose him. What's a little more— I'll really be able to move forward with him as my right-hand man. She glances over the Hiring Chart and makes a decision.]* Allen, I think I can make that work. Let me talk with personnel. I'll have to call you tomorrow since it's nearly five o'clock now.

ALLEN: Sounds good. If you have a minute, I'd like to take a quick turn through your general ledger system to get a better idea of what we're dealing with. Can you spare a little more time?

JUNE: Yes. *[. . . though the request surprised her. After 30 minutes reviewing the system, she was convinced that Allen's computer knowledge would be an asset to the department.]*

The next day June called and told Allen he'd get $71,000 with two weeks vacation to start and a third week after two years of service. To June's relief, Allen gladly accepted and asked June to send him a letter outlining the agreed-upon terms. She did. Allen was pretty pleased with himself. His old job paid $62,000 with a tiny bonus, so this position was a big move forward.

Let's analyze the negotiations process. First, Allen did his homework. He knew the salary range typically paid by employers in the field. Next, he thought through the reasons June, the hiring manager, wanted him. Using those and his own knowledge of the field, he put together a Hiring Chart. He called personnel to learn the details of the benefits package. He rehearsed his negotiations so he'd be comfortable asking for more and pointing out why he was worth that investment. He went to the meeting armed with tools and a strategy to persuade the employer to pay more.

**Men typically try to negotiate for more salary, while women generally accept what is offered.**

You'll remember that Donna, our female candidate, whom we discussed at the start of the chapter, accepted the job as offered. This means that Donna, the female candidate, started at $63,000, while Allen, the male, negotiated and obtained a starting salary of $71,000. That's $8,000, or 12%, more to start. All bonuses and future raises are determined from that starting base. Whereas Donna's bonus of 20% would be $12,600, Allen's would be $14,200 because his base is higher. Donna would be there for several years before she'd reach the $71,000 base salary. These

**The annual Working Women *salary survey* and the Department of Labor studies state women are still paid 23% less than men.**

are important facts to remember. Those who try to negotiate salary usually succeed. Often the only difference is that one candidate *asked* and the other candidate did not.

Women tend to accept things more willingly. They tend to devalue themselves and their work. They aren't as aggressive as men in their salary negotiations. So many women have written to me after reading my book (*60 Seconds & You're Hired!*) or attending my seminars to agree that they'd never negotiated salary. After using the salary negotiations I outlined, many of these women surprised themselves and got an increase. One woman, Martha, wrote to say:

I'd never negotiated for more salary, but your book and seminar encouraged me to try. I got offered a terrific job and didn't accept immediately. I worked on my Hiring Chart and all my persuasive arguments. When I went in the next day to discuss it and told them I thought their offer was a bit low, the employer offered me $3,000 more right off, plus a $2,000 signing bonus. I accepted it, but never even got to use my chart to make the argument. She told me, "We want you on the team, here's what we can do." The employer told me later she got really worried when I didn't just accept during her call. In the next 24 hours she put together the best package she could. She really wanted to hire me and get me to take the job. Wow! I'd never have believed I could do this, but it's sure gonna be fun spending all that extra money.

The first rule of salary negotiations is to *try*. In minutes you can find yourself thousand of dollars richer. (There's a complete formula for success I'll outline shortly.) Try—but use documentation and persuasive arguments such as Allen did and Martha was prepared to do. A strange transformation happens in the hiring process at the very end. The employer has often reviewed hundreds of resumés, interviewed the top choices, and narrowed it down to you. Once the employer decides you are the one, he or she ends the *selection* process. Now the interviewer moves to the *recruiting* process—selling you on the job and the company. At this point, employers or interviewers worry you won't take the job. Their panic increases. They want *you*. And they want to get what they want. Whatever it takes! Therein lies the secret power of negotiation: waiting until they want you, you, and only you. That's when the employer is most willing to pay more to get you. This is why it's important to leave all salary conversations until the job offer has been made.

## Dealing with Salary Issues

The first times you'll need to deal with salary concerns are likely to be when you respond to want ads that state "send salary history" or on job application forms. Applications are legal documents—never, ever lie on them. Any false statement (fudging up the salary) could result in termination if the lie is uncovered later on. I suggest you do not fill in the line requesting salary earned at your old job: Leave it *blank.* Our strategy to obtain the highest salary possible is never to mention salary before the employer does.

In a recent survey I conducted and sent out to 600 hiring managers nationwide, I found that 23% requested salary history as a part of their hiring process, most specifically in their want ads. Personnel managers and top executives all told us the same thing: Salary histories are desired to *screen people out* and to get a true estimation of the real level of job duties performed. That means salary information is used to *eliminate* you. Therefore, our strategy is this: Simply don't mention salary in your cover letter at all.

There are circumstances where employers' ads state, "Only those sending salary histories will be considered." Okay, our approach remains the same: Do not tell them what you made. Instead, offer the employer a salary range you expect to be paid. Cite an appropriate source, such as your trade association or a national salary survey, and state: "According to the American Hotel and Motel Association, the average salary for assistant manager at a medium-size hotel ranges from $25,000 to $40,000, and I'd expect to be paid in that range." This approach leaves the door open to future negotiation and puts you within a highly respected industry guideline. Additionally, you often don't know if a company pays below or above the average. So using a wide (but factual) range gives you a good playing field for later negotiations.

In my experience with clients and in conversations I've had with employers, the salary range has worked as a good alternative to the demand for a salary history. Still, the best option, whenever possible, is to avoid naming a figure.

Salary negotiation is a game—a sophisticated game— but a game nonetheless. Our goal is to obtain the highest salary possible for you. Waiting until the employer offers

**The first person to mention money loses.**

*Salary information eliminates those whose salary was too high, but more commonly, those whose salary was too low.*

the salary or salary range gives you the upper hand, and you can then deal from a position of strength.

## Handling Salary Questions during the Interview

The interview is where most people make critical and unfixable salary mistakes. Jeffrey, an engineer with two years' experience, interviewed for a job he really wanted. He'd been laid off from his first job and was eager to work again. During the interview the employer asked, "What were you making at the old company?" He responded, "$34,000." Not surprisingly, he was offered the job at $35,000. He called to discuss his situation with me. He wanted to be paid $41,000. The salary scale, he'd learned, went from $33,000 to $45,000. Jeffrey realized his mistake and said, "I'm dead in the water, aren't I, since I told them my old salary?"

I replied, "Pretty much, yes. You are not working, and this is equivalent to your old job. It's the only offer you have in your specialty. You can try to negotiate, but personnel is now involved and it'll be hard—if not impossible—to renegotiate now that they know exactly what you made."

"Can I fake it and allude to the option that I have another offer?" he asked.

"Bluff?" I said.

"Well, yeah," Jeffrey replied.

"I don't advise it," I told him. "Poker is one thing, but this is your future, and if they say 'forget it,' you've lost out on a real job. If you are willing to spend more time searching and feel this company's not great—then you can always walk away. So my question to you, Jeffrey, is this: Is it okay to lose this job and wait for another?"

"No," he concluded. "There's a lot I can learn here. I like the company. So I guess I just learned a very expensive lesson about salary negotiation, didn't I?"

Mishandling the salary questions during the interview can result in a lower starting salary or even being dismissed as a candidate. Let's slip inside the office where Lynn is interviewing for a grocery store manager position:

EMPLOYER: Lynn, what is the salary you are expecting?

LYNN: [*Lynn decides to use the Salary Extractor (see Chapter 4)*]
Well what is the range for this job?

**You establish your own bottom line.**

EMPLOYER: Depends on experience, but $45,000 to $50,000 is what we have in mind.

LYNN: [*Nods and says nothing.*]

EMPLOYER: Is that okay for you?

LYNN: I believe it's near my expectation. Of course, your bonus structure and benefits all weigh into the picture. I don't feel I have the complete picture yet of exactly what all your needs and responsibilities are. I'd like to proceed with the interview—I feel confident that we could settle on a fair compensation plan if and when you decide to make me an offer.

With that the employer moved on.

In actuality Lynn felt the salary was too low. The surveys from both her industry's regional and national associations stated the salary average for the position was $53,000. She did get an offer from this employer. They started the negotiations at $48,000 and ended at $50,000, but the bonus structure was also lower than average, so Lynn declined the job.

Her next interview a week later was with a growing company. Here's how it went:

EMPLOYER: Lynn, what did you make at your last job?

LYNN: It varied monthly, since I almost always made the bonus. What is the range you propose to pay?

EMPLOYER: We offer a range between $42,000 and $59,000, with quarterly bonuses tied to meeting sales quotas and performance goals. Typically, the bonus can be between $1,000 and $4,000 a quarter.

LYNN: I'm within your range.

EMPLOYER: Okay. [*The interview continued.*]

Lynn was offered the job and they settled on a salary of $55,000. Her decision to wait to obtain her true value proved to be worthwhile. In her case, Lynn had an extensive track record of past store management success and documentation to support her expectations. Waiting proved to be financially feasible and worthwhile.

Lynn was quite savvy in her approach to handling salary questions. This left a wider field for her to negotiate the extra income by moving to a new employer. Her old

CAREER COACH
tip

*Salary goals need to be based on solid facts and survey documentation, not just hopes, dreams, and entitlement expectations.*

salary had been $49,000, with bonuses averaging $2,500 to $3,000. She felt the first offer didn't provide enough incentive to leave. The second offer two weeks later did.

The Salary Extractor outlined in Chapter 4 aided Lynn in learning the true range the employer was willing to pay. By being noncommittal about her desires, she was in a stronger position to negotiate the salary once she was selected. The second employer's initial offer was $52,000. But when the employer was confronted with surveys that listed the average at $53,000, Lynn easily argued that her past achievements put her in the "above average" category. They quickly settled on $55,000.

## Who Can Negotiate for a Higher Salary?

The more years of experience and specific skills you acquire, the more leverage you have to negotiate salary. It's a fairly common practice for both mid-career and senior executives to open the door and negotiate a higher salary with the techniques I've outlined. But what about those just starting out or on the lower end of the pay scale? The techniques work whether you seek to make $500 more a month or $50 more. Many clients starting new careers (administrative assistants, LPNs, reporters, social workers, advertising account executives, dental assistants, and teachers, to name a few) have successfully negotiated higher starting salaries using this method. In the early years of your career, the most important consideration must be the opportunity to learn from a good manager as well as on the job. Sometimes, employers won't pay more for a worker—but it's still a good job to work at. If you try to negotiate, here's the advice I typically offer clients who have less than five years of experience: Keep your salary requests small. If you are offered $1,800 a month, $50 to $100 more is probably the most you can expect through negotiating.

If you ask for too much—$200 to $300 more a month—the employer may just dismiss you and say forget it (unless you have hot technical or other high-demand skills or credentials). Therefore, *a modest request is often a successful request.* You don't have much bargaining power early in your career. Another thing, many people's first few jobs may be with small employers. Typically, small employers (less than 100 employees) have a narrow pay range or no options to increase a job's salary scale. Therefore, carefully probe a small employer, resell them on how quickly you can make a contribution, and quantify your value as you realistically broach the amount you desire to be paid. Use the techniques I've out-lined, and you may obtain a few more dollars in your new paycheck.

## The Success Formula for Salary Negotiations

There are eight steps to follow that will increase your chances for suc-cessful salary negotiation.

### 1. RESEARCH AND DETERMINE YOUR TRUE MARKET VALUE

All salary negotiations must be based on facts, not assumptions. This step—often the most difficult—is essential for success. You must deter-mine a fair price for your services. To find the salary surveys and data you'll need, try these resources:

✔ *Reference librarians.* They can save time and effort by pointing you to the specific resources to use.

✔ *Books. The American Almanac of Jobs & Salaries* (Avon) by John Wright offers good information.

✔ *Associations.* National organizations typically do annual surveys by geographical regions.

✔ *Magazines. Business Week, Forbes, Fortune,* and *Working Women* often publish salary surveys of job-income averages.

✔ *National Business Employment Weekly.* The October issue has 50 different jobs and industries. Every week a different salary survey is published. For a back issue, call 800-JOB HUNT.

✔ *Want ads.* Employers often advertise a salary range. Reviewing the last six months of newspapers—local, plus the *Wall Street Journal*—can provide the basis of competitors' offerings.

✔ *Executive recruiters.* Most specialize in a specific industry and can provide salary ranges for the asking.

✔ *Internet.* Many surveys can be downloaded. Try http://www.job smart.org/jobsmart

✔ *Colleagues and friends.* They can offer insight into the ranges that competitors pay for the kind of job you seek.

### 2. ESTABLISH YOUR VALUE

Use the interview as a time to continuously reaffirm your value to the employer. Stress, with proven examples from your past, how you will be a key contributor. Focus on how you'll meet the employer's needs.

### 3. NEVER MENTION SALARY BEFORE THE EMPLOYER DOES

In this power game, you tip your hand if you offer your salary before the employer tells you the range or the exact figure the job pays. You should always speak in ranges, never exact figures.

### 4. QUANTIFY YOUR WORTH

Once the offer is made, ask the employer why you were selected. Listen closely to employers' main concerns. Your persuasive arguments center on what they tell you and everything else you've learned in the interview. Complete both the Influential Selling Points chart and the Hiring Chart that follow to have your ammunition ready. Continuously focus on how effectively you'll meet the employer's needs and excel at the job. Reassure the interviewer you'll be up to speed and productive quickly. Stress that in a short time you'll be a contributor.

### MOST INFLUENTIAL SELLING POINTS

1. _____
2. _____
3. _____
4. _____
5. _____

### HIRING CHART

| Needs | Contributions |
|-------|---------------|
|       |               |
|       |               |
|       |               |
|       |               |
|       |               |
|       |               |
|       |               |
|       |               |
|       |               |
|       |               |

The Hiring Chart is a powerful tool to give to the employer. He or she can review it and then show it to his or her boss or personnel. Often, the interviewer must go to a higher authority to get approval to give you a higher salary. This chart provides solid evidence and validates your persuasive arguments when it's passed on to upper management.

## 5. WIN-WIN APPROACH

Realistic expectations and a willingness to "settle" or "compromise" allow both parties to leave pleased and happy. Showing that you'll come down a little if the employer goes up a little is often the undercurrent to success, as it allows both parties—you and the employer—to walk away as winners.

## 6. KNOW YOUR BOTTOM LINE

Some organizations will negotiate salary. The higher your position, the more likely salary will be negotiated. Other employers, such as small businesses, may predetermine the dollars they can spend to have a job done. No matter how good you are, they will not (and in most cases don't have the money to) pay more. City, state, federal, and many non-profit jobs often have a pay scale that indexes job experience into a salary position with little more than a $1,000 to $2,000 leeway. Your decision must look at the whole picture. The company, the growth potential, the stress (or lack of), coworkers, training options, commute time, flexible hours, benefits, perks such as cars or free day care—all must be weighed by you to make a decision. You know what is most important to you—perhaps a few extra dollars weighed against a two-hour commute every day isn't worth it. Determine the lowest amount you'll accept, and be willing to pass on jobs below your worth, needs, and value. Sometimes, clients' financial situations force them to accept the first job offered. Then it's not long before they are again trying to plan a way to get a promotion, raise, or new (and better-paying) job. As I've repeatedly seen with my clients, you oftentimes turn down a lower offer, and a few weeks later the right—and better-paying—job comes along.

## 7. NEVER BLUFF

Ultimatums can result in offers being withdrawn. Never fib or bluff with an employer. "I have other offers" might get a response of "so take them." A confident, friendly, savvy team player approach is better.

## 8. PROMISES ARE NOT GUARANTEES

Many employers have selective memories and changing budgets. Promises of future bonuses and raises often disappear once you're on the job. A promise of a bonus after six months is negated when, three months after your arrival, a companywide letter states "no bonuses this year." Such a scenario would leave you with few options. Negotiate hard to get the money, benefits, and perks up front. Then get the agreement in writing. You can ask the employer for a letter or write it yourself and have it countersigned by the employer. Don't make it a big deal; a simple statement of facts like this guarantees exactly what all parties agreed to.

*Sample Letter of Employment*

---

Sept. 1, 1997

Dear Employer:                                                    CONFIDENTIAL

I'm happy to accept your position as your new counselor. We have agreed to the following terms:

Salary: $31,000

Hours: Mon.–Thurs. 8–5, Fri. 8–12; 36 hours per week
(one-hour lunch on Mon.–Thurs.)

Vacations: 1 day per month

Sick: 1 day per month

Parking: reimbursed by the company

Benefits: medical, 401(k), life, and disability as company offers

Starting date: October 17, 1997

I look forward to a long and successful working relationship. This letter of understanding serves as a binding agreement between Elaine Claison and Valley Counseling Center and its representative, Director Joseph Sanderson.

_____          _____
Elaine Claison                                Joseph Sanderson
Counselor                                      Center Director

---

Employment letters are necessary whenever you deviate from the standard company plan. In our sample employment letter, the client negotiated the reimbursed parking (a $65 savings per month). When she got her first check, this amount was not included. Without this letter of agreement she would have lost that extra, promised benefit. It seems her new boss didn't recall ever agreeing to the parking subsidy. A written letter alleviates a lot of potential misunderstandings down the line.

**Four Keys to Successful Salary Negotiations**
1. **Never mention $money$ first.**
2. **Continuously sell yourself and reiterate your value.**
3. **Ask a fair price.**
4. **Evaluate the whole offer against your long-term goals and objectives.**

## Multiple Job Offers: When the Whole World Wants You

Occasionally, a client is fortunate to have a job offer from one employer and then can actually create a bidding war by bringing in another employer. In one client's case, he received one offer and wanted to induce another, more desirable employer to also make an offer. This is tricky, as there are numerous factors outside your control. First, go to the other employer honestly and politely and say, "I've got a firm offer I need to decide on. I'm still very interested in your job. Can you tell me whether I'm still in the running as a top candidate or not since this information could influence my decision?"

Three answers can come forth:

1. *"No."*  Now you aren't betting on a dream.

2. *"We haven't decided."*  Ask for a timeline, but don't force the employer to meet your scheduled deadline. You may have to accept the first offer and play along with this other employer if the decision is weeks away. There is always the option of quitting a job a couple weeks after you start it to go to a better position if you get a later offer. This action won't win friends, but it does happen.

3. *"Yes, you are our top candidate."*  This answer requires you to nail down the employer's timeline. The employer may immediately counter with an offer.

By asking, you'll make a decision based on facts and not on hopes, hunches, or maybes.

One client, Lee, a computer systems analyst, had three offers. All had various components. One required relocation. I had him outline the offer of each by salary, benefits, and company, noting pluses and minuses. This helped to clarify the points of comparison. Since a move was involved, he added his wife's preferences as a factor to consider.

| | Company A | Company B | Company C |
|---|---|---|---|
| Location | Seattle | Seattle | San Jose, Calif. |
| Salary | $71,000 | $69,000 | $82,000 |
| Relocation reimbursement | N/A | N/A | $25,000 plus $5,000 on signing; one year of employment requirement |
| Stock options | Yes | Yes | No—privately held |
| Bonus | Bonus: up to 8% | 7–12% | Varied based on company profits (up to 20%) |
| Commute | 45 minutes | 15 minutes | Unknown |
| Company +'s and –'s | + Downtown<br>– Commute<br>– Weak bonus<br>+ Nice workspace | + Close<br>– Lower salary | – Requires move<br>+ Family in southern California<br>+ Nice workplace<br>+ Progressive company<br>– Cost of living 10–15% higher<br>+ Excellent salary and bonus structure |
| Wife (Ming Ly)—California move okay if money is worth it. | | | |

When Lee had a hard time deciding, I had him go see each employer again. That visit was insightful, as he learned more about the individual culture of each company. After that final stop, he felt the move to California was the best offer. He decided the move would indeed be worth it once the company agreed to help him with the sale and purchase of his home.

Compare; visit each employer again; then decide: Where would you best be able to use your talents? Your potential happiness is a key barometer in your decision-making process. Money does not always buy happiness. Make your selection after some soul-searching and careful thought and reflection.

# *Raises*

Julie, a credit manager at an electronics company, was nervous. Today was the day she would ask her boss, Mr. B, for a raise. She had to—she and her husband could barely make ends meet. She kept telling herself it would be okay. "I deserve it," she thought. Today was the day, no matter what. She'd put it off too long, and besides the anxiety was killing her.

Mr. B was having a bad day. And, for that matter, it been a tough six months. The company's sales were down. As VP of operations, Mr. B was under tremendous pressure to cut costs and speed up processing time. Each day got worse, not better. This morning the CEO had screamed—*screamed*—at all the managers for action. He wanted results or he'd be finding a new team. Mr. B was tired and frustrated today. His thoughts were interrupted when Julie, the company's credit manager, knocked on his door.

JULIE: Hi, Mr. B. I'd like to talk to you for a few minutes.

MR. B: Sure, sit down. [*I hope this is fast, thought Mr. B, I want to get out of here. It's Friday, almost 3 P.M., and she better not be dropping something big on me now.*]

JULIE: I've worked for Jameson Electronics now for seven years, but I have not had a raise in the last two. I think that being a loyal employee is worth a lot. My car is pretty old and Ken and I want to buy a new one. Cars are expensive, you know.

MR. B: Yes, they are. [*Not this now, Mr. B thought.*]

JULIE: I want a raise. I think that $200 more a month is appropriate. Everything else keeps going up—our rent, food bills, everything— and it's been 27 months since I've had an increase.

Mr. B felt angry. His first reaction was to tell Julie that he doesn't give raises so employees can buy cars, that she should take a money class if she couldn't afford a new car. ("Calm down and be cool," he told himself.)

MR. B: Why do you deserve a raise, Julie?

JULIE: Loyalty. Seven years—not too many people have been here that long. I think that's significant. [*Julie started to feel nervous and put out. Doesn't loyalty count for anything? They would be in a bind without me, she thought.*]

Silence.

JULIE: I've been in the credit area all that time, so I really know my stuff. And other companies are giving raises—I believe I deserve one, too.

Mr. B pondered a minute or two. Silence prevailed. Julie grew nervous and began to play with the ring on her finger.

MR. B: Julie, you know that the company's sales are down. We're looking to cut costs and consolidate. Today Bob was emphatic about lowering budgets. The time isn't right for a longevity raise. Last year at your review we talked about your computer skills. I recommend you take those Excel and database courses. I think you would be able to improve collections if you had a more sophisticated system. You haven't taken those courses yet, have you?

JULIE: [*Meekly*.] No.

MR. B: Okay then, unless I see an increase in your skills, more productivity, and quicker collections, I cannot justify a raise. Was there anything else?

JULIE: No, thank you.

Julie went back to her desk and grabbed her purse. She told the secretary she was ill and left. Inside her car, Julie started to cry. "He's so mean," she thought. "I deserve that raise—I do."

Mr. B sat back in utter frustration. "Employees just don't get it," he thought. "These are new times. Longevity isn't an asset—productivity is. The problem is, everyone wants more money, but few are willing to work for it. It's like every employee is suffering from an entitlement syndrome." He made a note to watch Julie's performance more closely over the next couple of months. If he didn't see improvement—and he doubted that he would—it might be time to replace her.

Four months later, when the company had to lay off some employees, Julie lost her job. Mr. B told her that her work performance had been marginal lately and she had been leaving early and coming in late. He was sorry, but she would get severance pay and one month of paid medical benefits.

Julie made some very critical mistakes. First and foremost, her timing and intuition on her boss's mood were way off. She picked the wrong day and certainly used an approach destined for failure. "Needing a raise" rarely encourages the employer to pay more. Companies in general feel that the salary is appropriate for the work being performed. Picking up new skills or going the extra mile is what most often influences the employer to pay more.

How can an employee get better results than Julie did? Let's look at Ken's case. He came to see me because I'd helped his brother negotiate a top salary when he landed his new job. Ken also wanted a raise. Here's what he told me:

KEN: I want your help in asking my boss for a raise. The corporation is facing some challenges, but I really like the company.

AUTHOR: Okay—let's discuss why you deserve more. What contributions have you made since you've been on the job?

KEN: Well, when I started two years ago, purchasing had some pretty old systems. I took several advanced courses, and since then I've really improved the system. Also, I worked with some of the larger contractors and asked for better deals. My predecessor wasn't very aggressive in that area. I think he liked just being entertained by potential vendors.

AUTHOR: What else?

KEN: That's it.

AUTHOR: What about the receiving and invoicing area. Did you make any changes there?

KEN: Well, yes, I did. That was another problem. We get over a thousand bills in a week, and receiving wasn't checking too carefully, so we were overpaying and double paying.

AUTHOR: How did you solve it?

KEN: I called Carl, the department head, and we set up a meeting. I told him we had to find some solutions together. We organized a team of my people and his. We called it "Progress Central"—and over three months developed several more efficient systems.

AUTHOR: Sounds good—what's happened as a result?

KEN: Well, we've speeded up our payment process. The receiving clerk can easily key in the shipment and double-check the order. It took programming an entire month to make it so easy a monkey could do it, but now it works like a charm. Those guys in receiving will skip the process if it becomes too time-consuming or a hassle. Anyway, payment is now made within 10 days of receiving, and the contract I negotiated calls for a 5% savings if payment is received within 20 days.

AUTHOR: Wow—that's great. How much did you save?

KEN: Save? I don't know, I never really figured it all out.

AUTHOR: Ken, we have to figure it out. If it's significant, there's the rationale for your raise.

KEN: I'll check the numbers once I'm back at work, but I'd guess it's been around $100,000 or more.

With that we planned Ken's strategy. We discussed the importance of his preparing the Hiring Chart I suggested (see Chapter 4). We also discussed, at length, the necessity to wait until his manager was in a good mood to ensure he'd be more receptive to the proposed raise.

It was three weeks before Ken made his pitch. Here's how the conversation went.

KEN: Hi, Bill, how's it going? Did Timmy's team win Saturday?

MANAGER: [*Smiling.*] He made a touchdown. He's really improved a lot—of course, gaining six inches and 20 pounds over the summer sure helped.

KEN: He'll be the next superstar—pretty soon the Dolphins will be calling. . . . There's something I've been meaning to discuss with you, Bill. Is now a good time?

MANAGER: Gee, I have a meeting at 10:00. If it won't take more than 10 minutes, sure. Otherwise, let's do it this afternoon.

KEN: Okay—I'll get with Kathy and get on your schedule sometime after lunch.

Four hours later . . .

KEN: Hey, Bill.

MANAGER: Ken, sit down.

KEN: You know, Bill, I've been with Paccar for over two years. I'm pleased to say I think we've made some important improvements while I've been here. Let me show you. [*Ken takes out his Hiring Chart and hands it to Bill.*]

## KEN'S HIRING CHART

| Needs | Contributions |
|---|---|
| **Purchasing processes and systems** | **Learned advanced Excel, Access, and FoxPro.** |
| | **Rewrote invoice process to simplify and computerize data. RESULTS: Saved 10 minutes per invoice.** |
| | **Created negotiations deal analysis model. Input each contract as it came up for renewal. Obtained new bids. Negotiated better terms. RESULTS: Reduced freight and warehouse charges, saved $12,700 (annually).** |
| | **Negotiated 5% discount on bills paid within 20 days of receiving shipment (see below).** |
| | **Competitive bidding reduced materials fees while maintaining quality with 25 top vendors, including Amoco, Simpson, Glenn Steel, Mitsubishi, and Todd. Savings from 1/96 to 1/97 was $1.2 million.** |
| **Reorganized the entire receiving/invoice ordering/payment process** | **Organized a committee with accounting and receiving.** |
| | **Developed new plan to improve process time to immediate retrieval, verification of received goods, and authorization of payment. Worked with programming to develop computerized, fast, and easy system. Beta tested system with Amoco deliveries. Worked out bugs and safeguards to avoid double payments and minimize employee theft. Implemented entire system conversion three months after first group meeting.** |
| | **RESULTS:** |
| | • **Saved 10 hrs/wk in accounting.** |
| | • **Speedy check-in caused no slowdowns in receiving.** |
| | • **Obtained 5% discount in 90% of cases (incorrect shipments account for most of the remaining 10%).** |
| | • **Total savings during 10 mos. of implementation (1 mo. with Amoco, 9 mos. with 20 other vendors) = $98,972.** |
| | **Projected savings over next two years with full vendor participation estimated at $237,532.** |

KEN: What I've done, Bill, is look at what the needs of the job are. I've cited three important areas where we've made significant improvements. I put them in chronological order because I wanted you to see the progress we've made.

First, the purchasing systems were old. No one had updated the computer processes. I was challenged myself, so I took advantage of some training through Catapult. I learned some pretty advanced macros, spreadsheets, and database stuff. Then I used them to create more efficient and faster systems in our office.

I also developed a "deal model." I think Jerry [*the former employee who held his job*] did a poor job negotiating deals with vendors. I computerized the terms of each contract as it became due. I could then easily review the terms. I've been rather successful in negotiating better terms for us. A constant complaint I kept hearing from vendors was how slow we were to pay the bills. After the seventh vendor pointed it out, I believed it to be a true problem. I looked into it. Indeed, receiving had to complete several forms and then send them over to accounting. I called Carl and Sue in accounting to discuss the problems. I told them that if we could fix this problem, I could negotiate a discount that would save the company a lot of money. I could get us a 5% discount if the bills were paid within 20 days of receiving. We agreed it was worth it to try. So I began to obtain those concessions, and our three departments formed "Progress Central." Well, you know the rest. We met for over three months, dragged in programming, and have created a system that's working like a dream. I did a calculation—since it's been up and running over the last 10 months, that 5% discount has saved us $98,972.

BOSS: Really, I guess I never thought about the ongoing savings—you're right, though, that is significant. Seems to me, though, that you each got a nice bonus for all your efforts.

KEN: We did, Bill, and I appreciated you noticing and rewarding that project's success. But, I've been thinking that the company hasn't properly reevaluated all my ongoing contributions. I negotiated, and still do negotiate, the contracts. It's been a tremendous savings—nearly 100 grand, and that's perpetual savings. I also took a lot of my free time to advance my computer skills and redesign our systems and create the contract model analysis. I feel that these contributions are reflective of a higher performance and that my compensation—my salary—isn't reflective of these new duties and functions I've taken on. I'm requesting that my salary and job be reviewed.

BOSS: A raise?

KEN: I feel it's truly warranted.

BOSS: How much did you have in mind?

KEN: That's up to you—what are these kind of contributions worth to Paccar?

BOSS: Give me a day or two to think about it.

KEN: Sure. It's Monday, and I'll get on your schedule for Thursday.

BOSS: Friday's better.

KEN: Friday it is. Thanks for the consideration, Bill. [*Ken leaves the Hiring Chart.*]

On Friday, Ken drops by for the meeting.

BOSS: Hi Ken, sit down. You know that budgets are really tight. I discussed this with Joe [*his boss*] and here's what we can do. The new fiscal year starts in three months. We can give you a little bonus now. At your current pay grade, we have little room for any raise. So Joe and I will work with HR and move you up to the purchasing manager tier beginning on July 1. That'll bring a $7,000 increase, so you'll be at $53,000 with a new title. I've arranged for a $1,000 bonus based on all the systems improvements—that'll take four to five weeks to reach your paycheck. Both Joe and I feel you've done an outstanding job here at Paccar, Ken, and this is long overdue.

KEN: [*Smiling.*] Gee, Bill, this is great. I appreciate your efforts—a promotion—I never expected that. Thank you. I'll be sure to keep working hard. There's more I can do.

BOSS: Great, I'm counting on it. Let's talk about all that next week.

Ken had really done his homework. He also presented his case with facts on his performance and quantified his value to his employer. At the time he got this promotion, the company's policy was to hold tight on raises. Ken's presentation enabled his boss to upgrade his job to purchasing manager, thus moving up the personnel step ladder to give him a raise he had truly earned.

There's also another avenue you could pursue to obtain a raise, as this client did. Debra heard me deliver a keynote address on career success. She made an appointment to discuss her situation. It seemed she really liked her job and all the responsibilities she undertook. Her employer was a nonprofit organization, whose cause she believed in. Yet she felt over the last year there that her employer had taken advantage of her. She admitted that she was to blame because she took on extra work. Here's what she told me:

DEBRA: The association has doubled in the five years that I've been there. I love the job, but it seems everyone keeps giving me more to do.

AUTHOR: And you do it. Am I right? [*Debra nodded.*] Describe some of your job duties in detail.

DEBRA: Of course. I oversee the major fundraiser and a dozen smaller specialty events, recruit all the volunteers, develop the sponsorships for both my projects and other fundraising events, plus I produce our quarterly newsletter.

AUTHOR: Debra, how do these duties differ from when you first started?

DEBRA: Five years ago?

AUTHOR: Yes—think back. What was your original job description.

DEBRA: I was hired to coordinate our two major fundraising events— one's in May, the other's in late October.

AUTHOR: You came here because you wanted to try to decide what to do. You've just revealed the best strategy of all to obtain a raise. Your job description has changed entirely during the last few years. You've taken on more responsibility and have contributed a great deal more than when you started. Many nonprofits and associations tend to simply accept these contributions without increasing the base salary. I think you can make a strong case for a raise and remain in your organization. If I hear you correctly, you don't sound like you really want to move on.

DEBRA: I don't, but they won't give me a raise. John [*her boss*] will say what he always says: "If you want a lot of money, move to the corporate sector. We are a charity, and funds for administration and staff are strained as it is." Believe me, we've all heard him say that on numerous occasions.

AUTHOR: Has he ever told *you* that?

DEBRA: No, but he says it often enough at meetings, and people have quit when he refused to give them a raise.

AUTHOR: Well, I think we can help you present a strong case, if you decide to try. First and foremost, though, is John pleased with your work?

DEBRA: Oh yes—my performance evaluations are always outstanding. My next one is in a month. But with budget cuts, no one is getting any raises this year. It's just depressing to think about it.

AUTHOR: Well, let me paint a picture of what you'd need to do. You and I could create a Performance Chart that shows your old job description, the new one, and highlight some of the major contributions you've made. You'd need to go to the library and research salary surveys—we need that information to make the pitch. Finally, we'd need to role-play the conversation you'd have with John and work on how to deal with his objections. You'll need good answers to "nobody's getting a raise" and his standard reply, "go to a corporation."

Debra decided to put in the effort. She called her association and got a current salary survey. She dug out her original job description, and we created the new one based on all the duties she was currently performing. She worked hard on role playing—dealing with objections or any kind of conflict wasn't too easy for her. We even discussed some relaxation techniques (breathe deeply, shake her hands and feet to release some nervous tension) to use before she went in to see John. We both agreed she should approach the subject at the end of the performance review. As expected, John was full of praise and her review was good. When he asked her about her assessment of what she'd like to do in the coming year, she used that as her opening.

DEBRA: Well, John, I've given a great deal of thought to that. When I started here I was originally hired as a program coordinator, but over the years it's really developed into a management job. I brought in a chart to show you. [*She then handed him her Performance Chart.*]

## DEBRA'S PERFORMANCE CHART

| Old | New | Contributions |
|---|---|---|
| 1992—Organized and coordinated all aspects of the two major spring and fall fundraisers (¾ time). | 1997—Coordinate all aspects of fall and spring major fundraisers, including sponsorship, marketing, and volunteer recruitment. | 1992—Events raised $251,000. |
| 1994—Coordinator of the monthly chapter events. Position became full-time. | Coordinate the monthly chapter meetings. | 1996—Raised $727,000 plus $45,000 in sponsor-paid administration and event operation costs. |
| | 1995—Recruit volunteers for all association events. | 1992—Attendance was 30–40. |
| | Head the entire corporate sponsorship program. | 1996—Attendance averaged 100–125 and included luncheon and speaker. |
| | Publish quarterly newsletter. | 1995 and 1996—Secured 100–150 people to work at events and on program during the last year. |
| | | Ongoing—recruit sponsors to cover funding costs. Secured free printing, hotel sites, prizes for all association programs. |
| | | 1996—Donated services and products totaled $45,000. |
| | | 1995 and 1996—Began a newsletter to supporters. Doubled direct-mail prospect list to 15,000. Edited articles and wrote the fundraising donation plea. Coordinated printing and distribution. |
| | | Newsletter campaign has raised $26,000 over the five issues we've mailed. Produces repeat advertisement for upcoming and special events without incurring additional mailing costs. |

DEBRA: You see John, in the beginning I was responsible for only the two fundraisers. I was working three-quarters time, and then we decided that I'd handle the chapter events, so I went full-time—I've noted that under the original description. As for the chapter events, they are a good place to begin. You can see they were small meetings when I started. Now we have a catered meal, a speaker, and have triple the attendance. As you pointed out in your review, the newsletter has proven to be a great idea and vehicle for us.

JOHN: Agreed. Where's this all leading, Debra?

DEBRA: [*Smiling.*] Well, it's become apparent to me that the association has doubled my responsibility and workload, and I have gladly done it and feel my contributions greatly impact our success. However, my salary base has never been adjusted. I got two cost-of-living raises, but I still make $32,000. [*She hands him a second sheet.*]

*CONFIDENTIAL*
**ASSOCIATION SALARY COMPARISONS**
**Program Managers**

| My job: $32,000 | | |
|---|---|---|
| **1995 Association Survey:** | **Coordinators** | **$22,000–$34,000** |
| | **Managers** | **$29,000–$50,000** |
| | **Directors** | **$45,000–$76,000** |
| **City Club** | **Kathy's position (similar in scope)** | **$39,500** |
| **Cancer Society** | **Bill's position (similar in scope)** | **$36,800** |

DEBRA: I've assumed that my job really falls in the manager level. I checked with both the Cancer Society and City Club, and they seem to be at a higher compensation level than we are. What I'm requesting, John, is for you to take a look at all this, and then let's discuss the possibility of a raise reflective of the management work I now do.

JOHN: Debra, you do a lot. You're one of our top people. No one is getting a raise this year. I thought you knew that.

DEBRA: I've heard that, but John I see this not so much as a raise but as a realignment of my job grade to match my duties—to bring my contributions and my compensation to a congruent level since the duties have really doubled.

JOHN: Nonprofits have meager budgets; there are no extra funds.

DEBRA: John, let's suppose that Kathy [*another office person*] took over my job. She's got the event experience, but she's not that good at selling sponsorships or recruiting volunteers, and she'd need an outside communications consultant to help with the newsletter—agreed?"

JOHN: Well . . . yes.

DEBRA: Okay—you'd end up spending more money or collecting less if you didn't have me making the level of contribution I do. I think this is really a job change to program manager, which covers the job and duties I now perform.

JOHN: [*Contemplative and quiet for a minute or two.*] Debra, how much exactly are you thinking of?

DEBRA: $3,000, and it'll be confidential. I won't tell anyone except my husband.

John was again quiet, contemplative, and did not give away his position.

JOHN: Let me think about it. I'll talk to you tomorrow.

True to his word, John asked Debra to come by.

JOHN: Debra, I discussed this with Mary [*chairman of the board*], and we both feel you are a valued and worthy employee. We have no budgets for a raise, so there will be no raise. I want us to be clear on that.

Debra remained silent. She knew the strategy was to quietly listen to everything John had to say, so she only nodded.

JOHN: Okay—no raise. We do see your point that the job has changed. We decided to restructure the position and change the title to program manager. That job will hold a salary of $35,000, and your new position starts on the first. Congratulations. [*He smiled as he extended his hand for a congratulatory handshake.*]

DEBRA: Thank you, John. Thank you.

As she left, she thought about what I'd said. It did indeed prove "impossible" to give her a raise. Her boss's idea—a new job title—was essential to deal with the current corporate policy. This new position and its reflective salary would be set accordingly. Debra had never been more proud of herself than she was at that moment. She got the promotion and a raise! She also used two strategies that worked well with John: the job-duties comparison charts and the salary surveys. Additionally, she presented a strong argument that if she wasn't there, the company would pay outside fees since the employee most likely to take her job lacked some of her acquired skills. She also remained quiet and let John have his say. Her persuasion got her exactly what she had earned and wanted.

## The Formula for Raises

*USA Today* reported in a national survey that last year 24% of all female workers and 20% of all male employees went to their bosses and asked for a raise. Were they successful? Unfortunately, 55% of the women asking failed. Men had somewhat better results. Of the men who asked, 59% got a raise. Learning the success formula *before* you approach your manager can greatly improve your chances to accomplish this goal. You won't jeopardize your career by asking at the wrong time and, most important, in the wrong way. Those who succeed have learned to use some important strategies and guidelines to advance their careers. Here is a summary of the important strategies and tools you need to use to obtain a raise, plus the failure approaches that won't work. As organizations face competitive and challenging times, raises will unlikely be guaranteed. Most will be negotiated and based on the contributions you have made. You'll need to be persuasive if you do hope to obtain a raise.

## Worst Ways of Asking for a Raise

✔ *I need the money.*   Your finances are *your* problem—not your boss's. This holds no bottom-line value to them.

✔ *But Sheila got a raise!*   Most bosses get infuriated by this argument. Perhaps Sheila's done a better job. Discussing other employees is unwise and often against corporate rules. It may have serious repercussions.

✔ *Threatening to quit.*   More than one boss has said, "Fine. Go."

✔ *Refusing to work overtime or do new projects.*   Insubordination can be grounds to be fired. Most employers react badly to being blackmailed—you may win a small victory, but quickly lose the war.

✔ *Whiny never works.*   This little-kid approach annoys managers and puts you in a childish light.

## The Raises Success Formula

✔ *Timing is everything.* Be sure to pick a time when your boss is likely to be receptive and more positive.

✔ *Do your homework.* Research your organization's policies and step grades. Look into whether or not your duties can be reclassified. Obtain industry salary surveys to support and validate your request.

✔ *Quantify your request.* Use salary surveys and job comparisons to support your suggested compensation level.

✔ *Provide proof.* Charts can be very persuasive. Use either the Hiring Chart or the Performance Chart to illustrate your growth, achievement, and depth of contribution.

✔ *Practice your pitch.* Role-play your request with a colleague or friend. Go over it several times until you are cool and comfortable with the request.

✔ *Overcome objections.* Identify the potential objections you think your boss is likely to make and prepare solid answers. Then practice dealing effectively with the objections.

✔ *Know your boss.* Adjust your request to your boss's personality and operations style.

✔ *Remain positive.* Expect that your boss will need to either think about your request or discuss it with upper management. Don't push it if there's no immediate response.

✔ *Tolerate silence.* People often are quiet when they are contemplating. Don't babble—wait for your boss to absorb what you are saying.

✔ *Convince yourself.* Know your value and that you are worthy of it. You must be sincere to be effective in your persuasion.

Your success must be validated. Use either the Performance Chart or Hiring Chart to create the evidence that quantifies your earned raise.

**Name:**

| HIRING CHART | |
|---|---|
| Needs | Contributions |
|  |  |
|  |  |
|  |  |
|  |  |
|  |  |
|  |  |
|  |  |

**Name:**

| PERFORMANCE CHART | | |
|---|---|---|
| Old | New | Contributions |
|  |  |  |
|  |  |  |
|  |  |  |
|  |  |  |
|  |  |  |
|  |  |  |
|  |  |  |

# When the Answer Is No

Not every single salary request gets approved, no matter how fabulous you are on the job. Your performance may deserve it, your efforts may warrant it, your accomplishments may support it, but still the answer is no. There are times when the best persuasion skills will not move the mountain. When that's the case, these observations may be helpful.

1. *That's all the job is worth.* When an employer evaluates the job, he or she often dictates the maximum that particular job is worth. The employer will pay no more and will replace the worker rather than up the compensation to get those tasks done.

2. *Small employers tend to pay less.*   Profits and gross income are typically less in small organizations. There may be limited budgets since the revenues are stagnant or falling, and the employer can't absorb the increase in overhead a raise will cost. These small employers would pay more if they could, but the reality is they can't afford to.

3. *Priorities.*   The company's goals and agenda may dictate using dollars for equipment or facility improvements instead of salaries.

4. *"A" for Effort.*   You tried. The company knows what you want and is watching. If you continue to perform and maximize your contributions, you may be rewarded down the line months, or even a year, later.

5. *You can always get another job.*   This is your ace in the hole. You can choose to move on. In my experience, most people land the biggest salary increases when they move to a new company. That is always an option for you.

# GO FOR IT!

## REACHING THE STARS

*A few times in an entire lifetime you are able to dream something so big, so outrageous, that it is simply just a fantasy. A hope. A desire. A want. A goal.*

*But then as you move on with a mission you forge a path that's beyond what most dream, want, or do.*

*Those incredible fantasies become less outrageous and actually probable.*

*Somewhere along the way you realize you can do it.*

*You can. You will. You must. Your happiness depends on it.*

*Settle for nothing less than your best.*

*You'll be amazed at what you can accomplish when you try hard enough.*

*—ROBIN RYAN*

Nothing is sweeter than the thrill of success. That moment in time when you win the promotion, the raise, or the new job. If you close your eyes, you can see it happening. You can *feel* that thrill, that excitement. You can almost jump for joy now as you clench your fists and push them out over your head with a giant smile, emphatically saying *YES!*

Obtaining your dream is a time for celebration. It's a victory in your professional life . . . a *win!*

There will never be another time like now. If you use these 24 hours you can—positively—change your life.

Today you can begin the work and action steps to achieve your dream. You can set in motion a plan that takes dreams out of the realm of fantasy and brings them closer to your everyday reality.

There's never been another you. And there never will be. No one can do what you can. Not in the exact same way you do. No other living person is exactly like you.

My purpose in writing this book has been to teach you persuasion tools and success techniques as well as to inspire you with the motivation to go after your dreams. *You can change your life. You can make it better.* You, too, can WIN!

You now know what it takes. You know the homework, the research, and the contacts you need. You have a clearer idea about the value of your talents and how you can truly meet employers' needs. By now you have an action plan that you are using to reach your goals. You have an arsenal full of tools: 60 Second Sell, 5 Point Agenda, Performance Chart, Salary Extractor, Productivity Monitor, Hiring Chart. All of these will aid you in achieving your goals.

I remember one client, Justin, who had lost his job. Derailed and disillusioned, he came to see me. The economy was terrible; his field was flooded with other professionals like himself looking for work. The world seemed as dark and gloomy as a gray November day. Justin had lost hope. He needed a job. I pointed out that what he lacked was know-how. He had to learn the best ways to get into the hidden job market. To identify his five top selling points. To seek out and meet employers he'd like to work for.

With his newfound direction, he put all his efforts into his success. "Visualize yourself in the new job," I told him. "See yourself going to the new office. *See it!*" Visualization can be a powerful anchor.

Next I told him he needed a supporter—a cheerleader, so to speak— one person who would cheer him on every step of the way. He selected his sister. From 1,500 miles away she faxed, e-mailed, and called almost daily with a simple message: "I believe in you. You can do it."

Finally, he got the call for an interview with the employer of his dreams. With just 24 hours, we honed his strategy and developed the 60 Second Sell and 5 Point Agenda. He went in and excelled during the three-hour interview.

He got called back. They were down to two candidates. He was focused on his goal: landing this job. A prestigious company . . . a challenging position with plenty of advancement opportunity . . . he wanted it badly. But he stayed focused and energized.

At last the call he desperately wanted came: "The job is yours. Let's meet tomorrow." He was so happy, he was downright ecstatic when he called me. We also discussed his salary negotiation strategy. The new boss was skilled at negotiations, but she wanted Justin to come to work for her. In the end, he got $75,000 and an extra week's vacation. Better than the job he'd lost.

He had achieved his dream. But Justin knew it wasn't the end—just the beginning of a new rise. A new time in his life to excel. About 12 months later the top job became available (his boss's boss's job). He was flattered to be considered but not surprised to be passed by. His efforts on the job were getting noticed. When his manager moved on four months later, that promotion was his.

Justin told me that it was my belief in him that made the difference. He credited the career advice, techniques, and tools as well.

We all need someone to believe in us and cheer us on. I can do that for you as your career coach. As you read this book, envision me talking directly to you. . . . I'll be an encouraging supporter telling you to dream bigger . . . you can get more. You *can* do it. Just keep going. Work the plan. You'll get it. Follow the techniques. Do the work—it'll be worth it.

Commitment is the final step to make a dream become a reality. With commitment comes action and the efforts to go on until you win. In my experience, lack of action and committed effort is often why careers stall and people fail to get jobs or promotions. Many times you need to work smarter, not harder. You need to use the tools that work. I've written this book as I conduct my actual coaching sessions. I've informed you about trends. I've taught you how to use valuable tools. We've even been inside employers' heads to get a firsthand view of how they think and act. All this insight is to no avail unless you apply it. I know you are ready to change and put out the energy to make good things happen in your life. I'm your biggest fan. Keep this book close at hand and refer to it as often as you need to.

Make this success pact with me. This commitment is to *your* success. I'll sign and seal it, so once you've written down your goals you'll know that this is a dream you *will* make come true.

**ROBIN RYAN INC.**
11834 SE 78th Street
Renton, WA 98056

Your name: _____     Date: _____

## COMMITMENT TO SUCCESS

I, _____ , will _____ on or before _____ .
      *Your name*           *Set the goal*         *Completion date*

I've committed to this goal knowing it will better my life and better me. I refuse to fail. No amount of rejection will stop me. I'm committed and will succeed.

_____
*Your signature*

I, Robin Ryan, career coach and author, support you in this quest and endorse your commitment to success.

*Robin Ryan*
_____
*Author, Speaker, and Career Coach*

Once you start to move forward, you'll be amazed at the results you can achieve. *Dare to win!* I'm right behind you—applauding!

# INDEX

# *About the Author*

One of the nation's foremost authorities on job search and hiring, Robin Ryan is the nationally acclaimed and best-selling author of five books: *Winning Resumés, Winning Cover Letters, Job Search Organizer, 60 Seconds & You're Hired!,* and *24 Hours to Your Next Job, Raise, or Promotion*

Robin Ryan has appeared on over 400 TV and radio programs, including *NBC Nightly News with Tom Brokaw* and *Oprah.* She's a frequent commentator on the national CNBC television network and is a regular feature on Seattle's KIRO-TV News and KOMO Radio.

A constant contributor to national magazines and trade publications, she's been featured in *Money, Newsweek, McCall's, Glamour, Good Housekeeping, Cosmopolitan, National Business Employment Weekly, Black Enterprise, Today's Careers, Journal of Accountancy,* and *Executive Strategies,* to name a few. She's appeared on the pages of most major newspapers, including the *Wall Street Journal, Los Angeles Times,* and *Chicago Tribune.* In addition, she writes a career column for the *Seattle Times.*

A licensed vocational counselor for 18 years, she has a private career counseling and resumé writing practice in Seattle. She holds a master's degree in Counseling and Education from Suffolk University, a bachelor's degree from Boston College, and is formerly Director of Counseling Services at the University of Washington.

A popular national speaker, she frequently gives motivational keynotes or seminar programs at conferences, association meetings, and colleges. She can be reached at (425) 226-0414 to inquire about speaking engagements or individual consulting.